MW01032563

UNDERSTANDING "THE CRAFT"

AND HOW IT AFFECTS THOSE YOU LOVE

FREE
FROM
FREEMASONRY

RON G. CAMPBELL

Regal

A Division of Gospel Light
Ventura, California, U.S.A.

PUBLISHED BY REGAL BOOKS
A DIVISION OF GOSPEL LIGHT
VENTURA, CALIFORNIA, U.S.A.
PRINTED IN U.S.A.

Regal Books is a ministry of Gospel Light, an evangelical Christian publisher dedicated to serving the local church. We believe God's vision for Gospel Light is to provide church leaders with biblical, user-friendly materials that will help them evangelize, disciple and minister to children, youth and families.

It is our prayer that this Regal book will help you discover biblical truth for your own life and help you meet the needs of others. May God richly bless you.

For a free catalog of resources from Regal Books/Gospel Light please call your Christian supplier, or contact us at 1-800-4-GOSPEL.

All Scripture quotations, unless otherwise indicated, are taken from the *Holy Bible, New International Version®. NIV®.* Copyright © 1973, 1978, 1984 by International Bible Society. Used by permission of Zondervan Publishing House. All rights reserved.

Other versions used are:
KJV—King James Version. Authorized King James Version.
NASB—Scripture taken from the *New American Standard Bible,* © 1960, 1962, 1963, 1968, 1971, 1972, 1973, 1975, 1977 by The Lockman Foundation. Used by permission.

Cover Design by Kevin Keller
Interior Design by Rob Williams
Edited by Deena Davis

LIBRARY OF CONGRESS CATALOGING-IN-PUBLICATION DATA
Campbell, Ron, 1953-
      Free from Freemasonry / Ron Campbell.
           p. cm.
      Includes bibliographical references.
      ISBN 0-8307-2383-8
           1. Freemasonry—History. 2. Freemasonry—Religious aspects.
      3. Spiritual warfare. I.
Title.
HS403 .C355   1999
366'.1—dc21   99-050376

1 2 3 4 5 6 7 8 9 10 11 12 13 14 15 / 06 05 04 03 02 01 00 99

Rights for publishing this book in other languages are contracted by Gospel Literature International (GLINT). GLINT also provides technical help for the adaptation, translation and publishing of Bible study resources and books in scores of languages worldwide. For further information, contact GLINT, P.O. Box 4060, Ontario, CA 91761-1003, U.S.A. You may also send E-mail to Glintint@aol.com or visit their website at www.glint.org.

DEDICATED TO THE

OF ABRAHAM, ISAAC

AND JACOB: THE GOD

WHO DELIVERS US

OUT OF EGYPT—OUT OF THE

LAND OF BONDAGE.

WITH SPECIAL THANKS TO

DARLA, MY WIFE AND COMPANION

IN THE JOURNEY,

AND TO OUR CHILDREN—

JOSHUA, CASSIE, BRIAN,

BRANDON AND BRADLEY—

FOR THEIR PATIENCE

AND FAITHFUL PRAYERS

DURING THE WRITING

OF THIS BOOK.

Contents

FOREWORD

It isn't news to Christians who have even modestly attempted to keep up with what the Spirit has been saying to the churches that we live in a generation—more than any other generation in recorded history—that is actively and systematically engaged in spiritual warfare. Even much of the terminology we now use, which is mutually understood by leaders, did not exist 10 years ago. The Body of Christ is on one of the steepest learning curves ever imagined, and the end is nowhere in sight.

Ron Campbell has entered a tributary of God's current river of spiritual warfare that is largely unnavigated. Among the books in the large library of contemporary works on spiritual warfare, this book on Freemasonry is one of the few dealing with what is being termed "occult-level spiritual warfare." Let me explain.

Early in the 1990s, members of the International Spiritual Warfare Network agreed that it would be helpful to distinguish three levels of spiritual warfare, even though each is closely related to the others:

- *Ground-level spiritual warfare,* dealing with the ministry of deliverance, or casting demons out of afflicted individuals.
- *Occult-level spiritual warfare,* dealing not so much with individual demons but rather with a more organized and coordinated attempt by the powers of darkness to

keep certain persons and groups of persons in bondage. This would include, among other things, Satanism, witchcraft, shamanism, magic, fortune-telling, Eastern religions and the like.

- *Strategic-level spiritual warfare*, dealing with confronting higher-ranking principalities, powers, rulers of darkness and territorial spirits who have the assignment of keeping whole regions or people groups or other larger social networks of individuals in spiritual darkness.

Resources on *ground-level* and *strategic-level* spiritual warfare have proliferated, but expertise on *occult-level* spiritual warfare has not been forthcoming in an equal measure. The reasons for this elude me, and no one I have asked about it seems to have a satisfactory explanation. But there is total agreement that serious work in this area is sorely needed if we are going to continue to push back the boundaries of spiritual darkness.

Ron Campbell is a godsend. For several years now he has focused the spotlight of research, prayer and spiritual discernment on one of the foremost agencies of demonic influence in our society—Freemasonry. There has been no question in the minds of knowledgeable leaders in the areas of intercession and spiritual warfare that Freemasonry is inspired and empowered by forces of the underworld. Deliverance ministers know well that Freemasonry characteristically provides entry points for many demonic spirits. In fact, my wife, Doris, who has been active in deliverance for 20 years, has said that more often than not the last demon to come out of a victim is a spirit of Freemasonry.

The Bible tells us that if we are ignorant of his devices, Satan will take advantage of us (see 2 Cor. 2:11). In *Free from Freemasonry*, Ron Campbell dispels our ignorance of Freemasonry. He reveals it for what it is—a blatant form of what I call hard-core idolatry. I cannot overstress the importance of this point. American Christian leaders are woefully weak in understanding idolatry for what it is.

One of the results of the widespread trivialization of idolatry in our churches has been to assume a neutral or even a benevolent attitude toward Freemasonry. I am appalled when I hear statistics on the number of pastors who are Freemasons and when I learn of the reluctance of some denominational executives to take action when they know it is present in their midst. Divided allegiance is the sin God hates the most. He clearly sees it as spiritual adultery. It is a blatant violation of the first commandment, "Thou shalt have no other gods before me" (Exod. 20:3, *KJV*). My prayer is that *Free from Freemasonry* will turn this tide around.

In my opinion, Freemasonry must be dealt with as a malignant tumor in the Body of Christ and removed as thoroughly and as rapidly as possible. Ron Campbell's work is a sane, well-researched and courteous treatment of a potentially volatile subject and deserves the widest distribution among conscientious Christian leaders.

C. Peter Wagner
Wagner Leadership Institute

CHAPTER ONE

WHAT IS FREEMASONRY?

*Freemasonry Builds Its Temples
in the Hearts of Men and Among Nations.*
CARVED ABOVE THE ENTRANCE OF THE HOUSE OF THE TEMPLE,
WASHINGTON, D.C.

*In him [Jesus] the whole building is joined together and rises to
become a holy temple in the Lord. And in him you too are being built
together to become a dwelling in which God lives by his Spirit.*
APOSTLE PAUL, EPHESIANS 2:21,22

I looked up into the deteriorated dome and gazed at the cracked
and peeling artwork. A painted golden chain encircled the
dome's lower circumference and connected many strange and
eerie symbols, including a skull and crossbones and the all-seeing eye. As I glanced around the room, most of what I saw was
equally unfamiliar to me: two pillars with globes on the top, tri-
angular-shaped tables, compasses and squares, more odd symbols and several allusions to the sun.

I remember thinking to myself, *Why have I come here?* Then I noticed something I recognized. It was a portrait of Simón Bolívar etched into the stained-glass window near the front of the room. Other leaders of this nation assumed their rightful positions in the remaining windows lining the walls of this unusual building.

I began to have an inkling as to why I had been directed to this place. My journey had begun earlier that day in the spring of 1992. Our small entourage of prayer warriors was positioned in the vicinity of the presidential palace in Caracas, Venezuela. We had come to this thriving metropolis on a prayer journey to link hands with the local church in praying God's heart, will and destiny over their beautiful nation.

I wandered into a museum and quizzed the curator, seeking historical information that might assist us in praying more accurately. After a few moments, possibly as a response to my constant barrage of questions, the gentleman made a puzzling statement: "If you really want to understand the history of my nation, you must pay a visit to our Masonic Lodge."

Masonic Lodge? I remember thinking, *What is that? And what historical significance could it possibly have to Venezuela, or any other nation for that matter?* Though puzzled by the man's comment, we set our course in the direction of the Lodge. Possibly there we would find some tidbit of information, a nugget of knowledge that would assist us in this strategic prayer journey.

We passed through the iron gates of the Masonic compound. Because it was under renovation, we were free to wander about.

Having viewed the dome and the history of Venezuela etched into the windows, I moved to an annex of the main building. Hanging on the walls were portraits of some of our own U.S. presidents! Once again more questions than answers tumbled through my mind. *What is Freemasonry? And does the answer to that question have anything to do with praying more effectively for individuals, cities and nations?*

Sometimes we don't realize the full import of the places and events into which God leads us. It was months before I realized how much God had been directing my footsteps that day. It was in that Venezuelan Masonic Temple, by the direction of the Holy Spirit, that I began to navigate the multifaceted labyrinth of Freemasonry (or Masonry). I had much to learn. Since then, this educational process has ushered me into Masonic Lodges in many nations. It has directed me to interviews with current and former Masons of every level and stocked my library with Masonic encyclopedias, ritual monitors (books of Masonic instruction) and Grand Lodge history books.

Consequently, over the past seven years I have grappled with and entertained answers to some very serious questions—the same questions you may be asking:

- What is Freemasonry?
- What goes on behind the closed doors of the more than 13,000 Masonic Temples in the United States?
- Is there more to this fraternal organization than meets the eye?

From the research I've gathered, it appears that good men, without realizing it, have submitted themselves to pagan gods when they have bowed their knees at the altars of Freemasonry. This statement may seem unbelievable to you, but please stay with me. If my findings are correct, Freemasonry is blatant idolatry, and the consequential curses attached to involvement in Freemasonry are dangerous if not deadly for both Masons and their families. It is my desire and the intent of this book to assist men and their families to break free from the bondage and curses of Freemasonry.

I will explain what I mean about curses in later chapters, but for now, relevant information is necessary for understanding; and understanding is key in our efforts to advance into this freedom. So let's begin our journey by investigating the information available to us from the Masonic Lodge itself. What do Masons say about their Craft?

GATHERING THE DATA

It was soon after my introduction to Freemasonry during my visit to the Lodge in Caracas, Venezuela, that I set my course toward information gathering. I began to visit Lodges throughout America, discussing the subject with Masons of every level. I gathered the colorful brochures freely distributed by the Lodges (more about this later) and began to identify and interview former Masons and family members of men in the Lodge. I spent long hours in public and private libraries across America, reading up on Freemasonry as well as ancient mythology. For research purposes only, I even began to collect books on this strange discipline for my personal library.

I did not, however, begin by reading books that expose the Craft—books that Masons refer to as anti-Masonic books. Quite frankly, when I began my research, I was so naïve about the subject that I didn't even realize others had already written on it. While I certainly don't recommend that you bypass these valuable resources, I believe that God was directing me, for a specific purpose, to older and more original sources.

Due to the serious nature of our subject and because this book will spur many of you to do further research on Freemasonry, I'd like to interject a couple of important concepts. First, please do not underestimate the importance and power of prayer when you undertake a research project such as this. It is important to be led by the Holy Spirit of truth. Don't launch out in front of Him in presumption nor lag behind in fear and doubt. Stay in step with Him, empowered by the faith that comes from consistent time in prayer and His Word.

During our information-gathering process, my wife, Darla, and I prayed, prayed and prayed some more! We also engaged others in praying for us. They still cover us in prayer.

Second, I've learned something about research. If you're a Christian and a researcher, you may have recognized it as well. There is a difference between research and Holy Spirit-led research. The first kind is dry and boring, which I experienced in some of my college courses. However, Holy Spirit-led research bubbles with life and revelation as He directs your steps to places, people and books. He touches your ears to hear and your eyes to see in "quickened" understanding. I've even noticed that my attention span and comprehension level seem to increase when the Holy Spirit is directing the process.

Let me assure you that printed material is out there and available to those with an interest in the subject. It simply takes time, energy and sometimes finances to unearth it. I've located books in the musty recesses of public and university libraries. I've availed myself of the libraries in more than one Grand Lodge. I've purchased books from private citizens, garage sales and New Age bookstores. I've also purchased books from many Masonic Lodges throughout America. I'm convinced that on more than one occasion Masonic books have even been delivered into my hands by what I refer to as God-ordained "divine appointments." Let me share one such meeting.

SANTA CRUZ RENDEZVOUS

Early in my research, while on a visit to Santa Cruz, California, Darla and I felt impressed to visit a New Age bookstore. While this is not a practice I generally recommend, we thought this might lead to answers to some specific questions we had regarding Freemasonry. After an hour of searching the floor-to-ceiling shelves amidst the aroma blend of coffee and incense, I leaned against a shelf and began to pray for direction. Although I had viewed the book spines of every dark subject imaginable, I found nothing specific on the subject of Freemasonry.

At that moment, an oddly dressed young man entered the store. He had a crystal-encrusted leather band around his head and another crystal embedded on the end of a wand he carried. He wore a jean jacket with more graffiti per square inch than many of the buildings I've seen in Los Angeles. After making a beeline to a shelf, he removed a book and tossed it onto the floor. He then knelt over it and began to chant as he waved the wand above it in a circular motion. Thinking this rather odd even for this establishment, I watched and wondered and continued to pray even harder.

As the young man turned, I noticed the all-seeing eye[1] etched on the back of his jacket. I approached him and interrupted his party. After introductions and comments regarding the symbol on his jacket and its possible connection to Freemasonry, I asked if he was aware of any books in this shop that might be of value in my research. He walked over to a shelf that spanned an entire wall and, without a moment's hesitation, moved two larger books. He then pulled out and handed me one of the first of many books on Masonry that are now in my library.

After a few more moments of discussion, the tone of the young man's voice changed and he began to manifest strange guttural sounds from deep within. I suddenly felt that God was releasing us to continue our journey. Would I have found this book without the assistance of this young man? I'm not sure. I simply relate this story as an example of how God has positioned me numerous times at certain places to receive books and information relative to my research of this secret society called Freemasonry.

CONFUSION AND CONTROVERSY

As I pressed on through the maze of Masonry, a fact became immediately obvious: Masonry is a very sensitive and controversial subject. In fact, there are probably few subjects more confusing and controversial than Freemasonry. In many families and churches it is a hush-hush subject.

Take our initial question, for example: What is Freemasonry? If you ask 50 people to render an introductory explanation of the Craft, you might receive an equal number of answers or interpretations. Many would have absolutely no idea what you

FREEMASONRY IS A MULTILAYERED,

COMPLEX ORGANIZATION WITH MANY

INTERPRETATIONS OF ITS ROOTS,

SYMBOLS AND RITUALS.

were talking about. Others would mention Masonic charities, such as the Shriner burn centers. Some might suggest that Masons are the funny guys driving their cute little cars or motorcycles in the annual parade. A few would inform you that several world leaders were Masons, including some of our own presidents. Others would bring up conspiracy theories and the New World Order. How can there be so much confusion on a subject where everyone is reading from the same page?

Actually, this is one of the reasons for the confusion. My research indicates that most people are *not* reading from the same page. In fact, many are not even reading the same book. Freemasonry is a multilayered, complex organization with many interpretations of its roots, symbols and rituals. There are many levels of accuracy, authority and understanding, even among Masonic writers. This is confirmed by various Masonic promotional brochures and certain Masonic internet websites, Masonic history books, encyclopedias and other books of Masonic interest. It is this multiplicity of definitions and perspectives that often ushers in confusion to the casual observer of the Craft. Most people are left in the dark with more questions than answers.

EXOTERIC VERSUS ESOTERIC

When you see Masonic information in the form of glossy brochures or beautiful booklets, it is usually surface-level information written with the public in mind. This information is easily acquired from your local Lodge or may be ordered from the Grand Lodge of your state. It is also available on many Masonic websites on the internet. When information, activities and rituals of secret societies are made public, or revealed to the common folk and the uninitiated, we refer to this as exoteric knowledge. For example, if you attend a Masonic funeral or cornerstone dedication performed by Masons, you would witness an exoteric ritual.

On a somewhat deeper level is the information that, for whatever reason, remains secret. This secret information is termed esoteric knowledge, or wisdom. It is occult knowledge in the sense that it is hidden, secret or only revealed to the initiated. It details the rituals that transpire behind the closed doors of the Lodge. You would not, for example, receive this level of information on a public tour of the Masonic temple. It is available only to those of its membership who have progressed through certain rituals or degrees. When I say degrees, I'm referring to the many levels of initiation the candidate may pass through in his search for Masonic "light." All men must enter Freemasonry the same way; that is, they all pass through the Blue Lodge, or the first three degrees, to become a Master Mason. The Mason may then choose to continue his Masonic journey by advancing through the 33 degrees of the Scottish Rite or through the degrees of York Rite Masonry.

Even deeper yet, there appear to be levels of esoteric erudition within the Craft. What the candidate of the lower degrees is told is not necessarily the full explanation he may receive in the higher degrees. What is revealed in the ritual monitors is not always the same as stated in the Masonic history books and encyclopedias. And so the confusion and controversy continues, not just among non-Masons, but among Masons as well.

Taking into account the many levels of Masonry, you may now realize why our question, What is Freemasonry? is easily asked yet more difficult to answer. Let's continue our quest by perusing a few of the attractive websites and glossy brochures produced by the dozens of Grand Lodges.

ON SITE FOR INSIGHT

Even a casual surfing of the internet will reveal the large number of Masonic-interest websites. When I logged on recently, there were 483 such sites, and this number is growing daily. While the internet is a great place to begin your search, I must caution you on a couple of items. First, do not assume that everything you view on the net regarding Masonry, particularly who's who lists on all anti-Masonic websites, is accurate. Second, keep in mind that most of the information you glean from Masonic websites is exoteric. It is specifically crafted for a curious public. With this in mind, let's visit those sites designed and maintained by Grand Lodges.

As I accessed the Grand Lodge (GL) sites, I noticed that one of the first questions addressed happened to be the one we're asking, "What is Freemasonry?" The general answer posted by the different GLs varied little from site to site.

Making Good Men Better

The GL of Pennsylvania states:

> Its [Masonry's] singular purpose is to make good men better. Its bonds of friendship, compassion and brotherly love have survived even the most divisive political, military and religious conflicts through the centuries. Freemasonry is neither a forum nor a place of worship. Instead, it is a friend of all religions which are based on the belief in one God.[2]

The GL of England informs us:

> Freemasonry is one of the oldest secular fraternal societies. Freemasonry is a society of men concerned with moral and spiritual values. Its members are taught its precepts by a series of ritual dramas, which follow ancient form and use stonemasons' customs and tools as allegorical guides.[3]

The Grand Lodge that maintains this particular website then attempts to disarm the curious public regarding the sensitive issue of Masonic secrecy. It states:

The secrets of Freemasonry are concerned with its traditional modes of recognition. It is not a secret society, since all its members are free to acknowledge their membership and will do so in response to inquiries for respectable reasons. Its constitutions and rules are available to the public. There is no secret about any of its aims and principles. Like many other societies, it regards some of its internal affairs as private matters for its members.[4]

The conclusion of the article on this website encourages the Mason "to do his duty first to God, (by whatever name he is known), through his faith and religious practice."[5]

The website of the Missouri Masonic Lodge of Research provides us with more "facts" that the Lodge wishes to share with the general public. On this site we are told that "freemasonry teaches the universal principle of unselfish friendship and promotes those moral precepts which are in keeping with all great faiths."[6] As I viewed this site I noticed this creed was sandwiched between colorful symbols of many of the world's living religions.

And so it continues, site after site, promoting the seemingly positive aspects of membership in a secret society that purports to make good men better. Who were some of the men Freemasonry claims to have made better?

Famous Freemasons

Unlike the websites, Masonic promotional brochures provide hard copy that can be passed from friend to friend, enticing good men to join the brotherhood. In fact, *Friend to Friend* is the title of an engaging brochure whose cover depicts famous Freemasons. It is copyrighted by the Right Worshipful Grand Lodge of Free and Accepted Masons of Pennsylvania and informs us not only of Freemasonry but also of those who compose the group called Freemasons.

Many of our nation's early patriots were Freemasons, as well as thirteen signers of the constitution and fourteen presidents of the United States, beginning with George Washington.

Today the more than four million Freemasons around the world come from virtually every occupation and profession. Within the fraternity, however, they all meet as equals. They come from diverse political ideologies, but they meet as friends. They come from every religious belief, but they all believe in one God.

One of the most fascinating aspects of Freemasonry has always been: how so many men, from so many different walks of life can meet together in peace, never have any political or religious debates, always conduct their affairs in harmony and friendship, and call each other "Brother."[7]

Recently I received a call from a friend who loves music. She was very disappointed to discover that Mozart had been a Mason and that he wrote *The Magic Flute* for a Masonic degree. Others, who love Western movies, have shared their near disbelief that John Wayne was a Mason. I have in my personal library a set of books titled *10,000 Famous Freemasons*. I can assure you that if you leaf through its pages, you too will find a famous person you admire who was involved in the Masonic Lodge.

While Freemasonry is an organization, Freemasons are human beings; they are men. It is critical to distinguish the two. I believe that God does and that He feels quite differently about the two, as I will clarify later in this book. Think of it this way: A Mason could be your neighbor, your postman, your mayor or even your pastor. He could be your father, grandfather or uncle. You might even be a Mason yourself. Whoever the Mason in your life might be, I can assure you of this: God deeply and eternally loves him.

Masonic Philanthropy

The brochure *Friend to Friend* not only addresses who Masons are but also what Masons do.

> Freemasons are respectable citizens who are taught to conform to the moral laws of society and to abide by the laws of the government under which they live. They are men of charity and good works. They remain unchallenged as "the world's greatest philanthropy!"
>
> The Freemasons of America contribute more than one million dollars every day to charitable causes which they, alone, have established. These services to mankind represent an unparalleled example of the humanitarian commitment and concern of this unique and honorable Fraternity.[8]

Again, the Masonic brochures reveal only the exoteric, or public, activities of Masonry and not what Masons do behind the closed doors of the Lodge. Some suggest that Masonic philanthropy is merely the whitewashed tomb concealing the idolatrous death within Masonry's arcane chambers.

If you've toured a Masonic temple, you may have encountered the mysticism and secrecy within its hallowed corridors. You may also have noticed as I did that what is posted on the websites and printed in the brochures is what your guide echoed as you followed him through the Lodge.

I remember how puzzled I was when I first visited a Lodge and was told, "Ron, we are not a secret society, but a society with secrets." As I left, I knew that I had not penetrated the depths of anything secret but had viewed only what my guide had intended for me to see. I was certain there had to be more.

GOING DEEPER

Certainly much of the information that appears on the Masonic websites and promotional brochures is admirable. One could almost see why a man would desire to join the Lodge, particularly if this was the only data upon which he based his decision. But let's be honest. Would this information suffice to direct the steps of a young man to the Lodge doors?

Granted, to learn that many of our nation's heroes were Masons might serve as a drawing card. Don't we all want to be associated with successful men? Masonry states that it is an organization "making good men better," and I've yet to meet a good, honest man who doesn't aspire to become better. But even so, is this really what Masonry is all about? Or is there more to it than what I was led to believe as I toured many of the Scottish Rite temples and Grand Lodges of America?

Masonic author W. L. Wilmshurst, in his book *The Meaning of Masonry,* suggests there *is* more to this fraternal organization. He says there are "Mysteries" to be attained.

It is absurd to think that a vast organization like Masonry was ordained to teach to grown-up men of the world the symbolical meaning of a few simple builders' tools, or to impress upon us such elementary virtues as temperance and justice—the children in every village school are taught such things; or to enforce such simple principles of morals as brotherly love, which every church and every religion teaches; or as relief, which is practiced quite as much by non-Masons as by us; or of truth, which every infant learns upon its mother's knee. ...*Surely then it behooves us to acquaint ourselves with what that larger end consists...and to ascertain what are those "mysteries" to which our doctrine promises we may ultimately attain* if we apply ourselves assiduously enough to understand what Masonry is capable of teaching us[9] (italics mine).

My research corroborates Wilmshurst's comments: There is more to Masonry than meets the eye. My disagreement with this Masonic writer, however, lies in the value of the "mysteries" and their effect upon individual Masons and their families.

Before we draw hasty conclusions, however, let's talk to a few Masons and ex-Masons who have embraced the mysteries of Freemasonry. Why did they join the Lodge, and why have they now left the Lodge?

Notes
1. A representation of Osiris—the chief deity of ancient Egypt. See chapter 3 for more information on the legend of Osiris.
2. Right Worshipful Grand Lodge of Free and Accepted Masons of Pennsylvania, *Friend to Friend* (Grand Lodge of Free and Accepted Masons of Pennsylvania, 1994), brochure.
3. *What Is Freemasonry?* (This is the text of a leaflet published by the Board of General Purposes of the United Grand Lodge of England, 1984), website of the Grand Lodge of England.
4. Ibid.
5. Ibid.
6. From the website of the Missouri Masonic Lodge of Research, 1998.
7. Right Worshipful Grand Lodge of Free and Accepted Masons of Pennsylvania, *Friend to Friend*, brochure.
8. Ibid.
9. W. L. Wilmshurst, *The Meaning of Masonry* (New York: Gramercy Books, 1980), pp. 21, 22.

CHAPTER TWO

WHY MEN JOIN THE LODGE

Mystic Tie—that sacred and inviolable bond which unites men of the most discordant opinions into one band of brothers, which gives but one language to men of all nations and one altar to men of all religions, is properly, from the mysterious influence it exerts, denominated the Mystic Tie; and Freemasons, because they alone are under its influence, or enjoy its benefits, are called "Brethren of the Mystic Tie." [1]

ALBERT MACKEY,
AN ENCYCLOPEDIA OF FREEMASONRY

Do not be yoked together with unbelievers. For what do righteousness and wickedness have in common? Or what fellowship can light have with darkness? What harmony is there between Christ and Belial? What does a believer have in common with an unbeliever? What agreement is there between the temple of God and idols?

APOSTLE PAUL, 2 CORINTHIANS 6:14-16

Decisions, decisions! What do I want to be? Where should I attend college? Who will I marry? Should I marry? We've all echoed similar words, if not verbally, at least mentally. Like water flowing beneath the bridge of time, the passing years and experience have taught me just how important making the right decisions can be. Unfortunately for most of us, education comes as we sort through the consequences of our wrong decisions. Aren't you glad God heals and restores?

One of the decisions that hundreds of thousands of young men will make—particularly if they exhibit leadership qualities—is to align themselves with a fraternity, which is a group of people associated, or joined by, similar backgrounds, occupations or levels of interest. These fraternal organizations may include a high school order such as DeMolay or one of the dozens of Greek fraternities in college. Even later it may be the Masonic Lodge.

What would influence a man to align himself with a fraternity, particularly with Freemasonry? Are there certain drawing cards, perks or benefits?

BENEFITS OF THE BROTHERHOOD

After teaching the closing session of a conference in Florida, I was met at the front of the church by a Mason and his wife. He requested that I pray for him, so we knelt at the altar. I asked for specific direction on how I might assist him and he whispered, "I would like to repent for my involvement in Freemasonry."

Before I could respond, he immediately broke into a prayer of repentance. "God, please forgive me! I thought Masonry was one of the few things in my life that I was doing right. I'm so sorry for my involvement in the Lodge." His prayer continued for a few more minutes with his loving wife kneeling beside him and praying in agreement.

Please understand that I respect the privacy of this gentleman and his prayer as intimate communication between him and God. I am sharing his opening statement because it confirms something you need to know: Most men do not join lodges of Freemasonry with the thought that it is anything less than good and right. In fact, most men know little about the Lodge when they join. They are simply convinced by friends, fathers, fathers-in-law, uncles or grandfathers that it is a good thing and would benefit them greatly. They are persuaded by the apparent mutual benefits of the brotherhood.

PROTECTION AND ASSISTANCE

Many Masons cite protection and assistance as a benefit they have received or hope to receive for joining the Lodge. For example, membership grew during seasons of war. It seems there was a bond, what Masons call the Mystic Tie, that united Freemasons even from opposing sides of military conflicts.

In the nineteenth century, with the dark days of the Civil War draped across young America like grave clothes, we see the Mystic Tie in action. As General W. T. Sherman drew near certain towns, the firebrands of his troops cast eerie shadows on some very unlikely handshakes. I first became aware that these bizarre meetings had taken place as I walked and prayed along Sherman's 800-mile trail of destruction through Georgia and the Carolinas.

It was the fall of 1996, and I had been asked to assist Gene Brooks and Christian Bass, codirectors of Operation Restoration, on a strategic prayer journey of repentance and reconciliation. We had marched for six days when we entered the small, quaint town of Sandersville, Georgia. As is the case in most small Southern towns, the local Masonic Lodge and the courthouse were located near the town square. On a commemorative placard at the Lodge I read these astonishing words:

Masonic Temple

A beautiful reproduction of the Greek Temple Athene, erected in 1855-56 for the Masons, of brick, handmade by slaves, stood on this corner. An appeal by Mr. James D. Anthony and Dr. James R. Smith —Methodist Ministers—and Mr. Pincus Happ, members of Haynes Chapter of Royal Arch Masons, saved the building from destruction by Sherman's Army in 1864, when all other public buildings in town were burned. This was one of several Masonic Temples in Georgia spared by Union officers who were Masons.

In other words, the Union officers burned all the buildings, even the churches, yet spared the Masonic Lodge simply because of the Mystic Tie of Masonry.

We are informed by Masonic sources of a legend in connection with a famous battle that took place near Houston, Texas. After the battle of the Alamo, Sam Houston and Stephen Austin, both Masons, finally confronted General Santa Anna and his troops in the battle of San Jacinto. The Mexican troops were being slaughtered and the general found himself in the throes of death. In what was possibly a last-ditch effort to preserve his life, he gave the Grand Hail, or Masonic distress signal, and his Masonic brothers, though on opposing sides of the battle, spared his life. I've seen the spurs that General Santa Anna supposedly wore that day. They are enshrined in the George Washington National Masonic Memorial museum in Alexandria, Virginia.

On a recent ministry trip to the South, I took a few minutes to steal away to the local Masonic Lodge to once again ask a Mason why he had joined Freemasonry. I spent 45 minutes with George (not his real name), a kind elderly man who was a Past Master and current secretary of his Lodge. George said:

> It was at the beginning of World War II, and I had just graduated from high school. I went to the funeral of my grandmother and was approached by a couple of my uncles who told me I should consider joining the Masonic Lodge. They said that no matter where I went in the world, particularly during the war, Masons would be there to assist me. And when I returned, they would also help further my career.

George, like many other Masons with whom I've conversed, had decided to join the Lodge simply because it seemed best for his future.

The desire for security and assistance by brother Masons was not limited to times of war. Ex-Mason Charles Finney also admits to this inducement of assistance:

> I know something about it, for I have been a Freemason myself. Soon after I was twenty-one years of age, and while in Connecticut at school, an old uncle of mine persuaded me to join the Freemasons, representing that, as I was from home and much among strangers, it would be of service to me, because if a Freemason I should find friends everywhere.[2]

I have listened to those in the Lodge who said they joined Freemasonry not just as a present source of security for themselves but as a future source of security for their loved ones as well. As with many fraternal organizations of the nineteenth century,

Masonry boasts that one of its founding purposes was to assist the widows and orphans.[3] I've walked the manicured lawns of more than one senior citizens' center owned and operated by Freemasons.

FINANCIAL BENEFITS

Freemasonry seems to attract businessmen. The founders and CEOs of many large businesses and corporations are Masons. Most Masons agree that this fraternity is a great place to network and provides key business contacts for them. Though men theoretically are not encouraged to join the Lodge for this reason, many of the candidates for initiation realize the financial benefits and the rights and privileges that flow within the alliance of this brotherhood. The "grips and phrases" (hand signals and code words) of men in this secret society open doors of opportunity that would normally remain shut.

One morning, as I sat down at my desk, I found a page torn from the telephone book. Our son Joshua had noticed it while leafing through the yellow pages and thought I would be interested in the graphic, so he tore it out and saved it. It was a three-inch by three-inch advertisement of a service company. Superimposed on the background was the Masonic Compass and Square symbol. To the casual observer it would have remained undetected, but Masons of all levels recognize the significance of these symbols. This was the business of a fellow Mason, no longer to be regarded as just any other potential business relationship. This symbol would alert fellow Masons to a previously established alliance, forged by the mysterious handshakes of brothers behind the closed doors of the local Lodge. The fiscal benefits of this kind of brotherhood are difficult to abandon, as a businessman I'll call Mark could attest.

When I met with and ministered to Mark, a Freemason, both his marriage and finances were in complete disarray. Mark felt that this secret society he belonged to had opened him up to less than God's best for him and his family, and he decided to demit (or resign) from Freemasonry. However, though he stopped attending the Lodge, he continued to pay his dues.

Early in our discussion I realized that Mark was on a "merry-go-round" with one foot on and one off. The extreme fear and friction of his divided heart were tearing him apart. He feared not only losing customers if he quit paying his dues, but also answering his Masonic friends about why he had left the Lodge. As we continued to talk, Mark realized that he had allowed the "benefits of the brotherhood" to continue to influence key issues in his life. He decided it was now time to make the complete break.

POLITICAL ADVANCEMENT

In addition to citing protection and financial opportunities as reasons for joining the Lodge, other Masons have stated that they joined for political interests. It's no secret that many of our elected officials are Masons. They hold offices in the federal, state and local governments and are positioned both in the House and the Senate. They are also seated on the benches of our judiciary system.

> From 1789 to the present, there have been 108 Justices of the United States Supreme Court. Depending on which source is consulted, 34, 36, 38 or 40 of them have been Freemasons. This means about one-third of the Supreme Court Justices were Masons.[4]

Masons have also repeatedly occupied the desk in the Oval Office. At least 13, and possibly as many as 17, of our presidents have been Masons.

THE SOCIAL SIDE

With the valuable assistance of Reverend Harmon Taylor, international director of HRT Ministries, the ministry of Jeremiah Project conducted a survey in the summer of 1998. This survey was sent to ex-Masons throughout the United States in an attempt to better understand why men join Freemasonry and why they resign, or demit. This particular questionnaire, though somewhat limited in scope and size, revealed a common reason why those surveyed joined the Lodge. It was because relatives or men they trusted had asked them to join. When asked the question, What attracted you to Freemasonry? here were a few of their responses:

- My father belonged [to the Lodge]. Also, the people who belonged were pillars of the community—leaders and influential people I admired.
- I believed I would fellowship with men doing good deeds.
- I've always heard it was a good social activity for men.
- My brother-in-law was a Mason and told me that it was a good thing.

Others I have interviewed have confirmed that they too were simply looking for a social organization of reputable men within the community with whom they could fellowship.

MASONIC CHARITY

Masonic literature informs us that Masons raise hundreds of thousands of dollars, if not millions, on a daily basis for children's hospitals, burn centers and medical research.

While visiting my sister in a Colorado hospital, I bumped into some Shriners. All Shriners are higher-level Masons. In our discussion they informed me, as others have on numerous occasions, that they joined the Lodge for charitable reasons. Usually when I'm listening to men who cite this motive, I hear a verbal ledger of monetary inflows and outflows of Masonic charities.

THE MYSTERIOUS NATURE

Some Masons admit that they were intrigued with the aura of mystery that permeated the Masonic Lodge. There's something about being on the inside of a secret. "The mysterious nature of Masonry was one of the things about it that attracted me," states Jim Shaw, former 33rd degree Mason and cowriter of the excellent book, *The Deadly Deception.*[5]

Though most men join for somewhat honorable reasons, I've also talked to those who sought out Freemasonry for its occult nature. While teaching and researching on the West Coast last year, I met with the historian/librarian of a Masonic Lodge. He was young, bright and energetic, and what he said caught me off guard. He equated his joining Freemasonry with furthering his education in the occult. He then tried to encourage me to seek out the benefits of Masonry's occultic arts. He directed me to a local bookstore where he said I could purchase my own set of Tarot cards, primers on the Cabala (Jewish mysticism) and books on the Ancient Mystic Order of the Rosicrucians (a religious movement devoted to esoteric wisdom with emphasis on psychic and spiritual enlightenment).

The Mystic Tie

As previously stated, most of the reasons for men to join the Lodge seem to be honorable. On the surface, at least, Masonry appears to be somewhat benevolent. But what of the "Mystic Tie" that unites men of all nations and gives one altar to men of all religions? Shouldn't this be a little disconcerting to a Christian man who is admonished by the apostle Paul to "not be yoked together with unbelievers?" (2 Cor. 6:14). Is it possible that in ignorance, millions of unsuspecting young men who have bowed at the strange altars of Freemasonry have yoked themselves with wickedness rather than righteousness, darkness rather than light, and idols rather than the living God? I believe they have.

IT'S NOT AN ISSUE OF INTELLECT OR HIGH POSITION IN THE COMMUNITY THAT SHIELDS US FROM DECEPTION, PARTICULARLY IF THAT DECEPTION INVOLVES SPIRITUAL MATTERS.

Unfortunately, even great men have been deceived into unholy alliances or engaging in rituals that are less than good. You see, it's not an issue of intellect or high position in the community that shields us from deception, particularly if that deception involves spiritual matters. If ever there was a man of wisdom, wealth and high position, the Scriptures inform us it was King Solomon. Yet Solomon, in all his wisdom, bowed at foreign altars and embraced wickedness instead of righteousness, and idols rather than God.

Many ministers and theologians suggest that the pagan altars of the ancient Middle East are not unlike the altars that

Freemasons bow at today in Masonic Lodges throughout the world.

Though millions of good men join the Lodge for honorable reasons, that doesn't make the Lodge good. Thousands of people would even agree that Freemasonry does not make good men better. Rather, it is injurious to the cause of Christ in the lives of those who join the Lodge. I have letters in my personal files that will never be read by the public at large. They are the personal cries of family members whose loved ones joined the Lodge and the expressions of regret by former Masons who bowed their knees at the altars of Freemasonry.

Over the past two-and-a-half centuries, thousands of individuals, church leaders, Christian denominations and prominent evangelists have addressed the issue of Masonry's deadly deception. Edmond Ronayne, author of *Edmond Ronayne's Handbook of Freemasonry*[6] and former Worshipful Master of Keystone Lodge No. 639, writes:

> In all the popular Manuals of Freemasonry and in its standard works of the highest authority and merit, there are four well-authenticated claims as set up on behalf of that institution, as follows:
>
> First, that it is a religious philosophy, or a system of religious science. Second, that it was revived in its "present outward form" in 1717. Third, that all its ceremonies, symbols, and the celebrated legend of Hiram in the Master Mason's degree were directly borrowed from the "Ancient Mysteries," or the secret worship of Baal, Osiris or Tammuz. And finally, that a strict obedience to its precepts and obligations is all that is necessary to free man from sin and to secure for him a happy immortality.[7]

Could the filed letters of regret from ex-Masons and personal cries of family members be directed at the same organization promoted in the glossy brochures and websites we visited in chapter 1? What does Ronayne mean when he says Masonry's symbols are borrowed from the Ancient Mysteries, or the secret worship of Baal and Osiris? Is he justified in his stinging declaration regarding a society through whose doors many of our forefathers have passed? Why would this manner of criticism be leveled at an organization that professes to "make good men better"?

If the doors to a Masonic temple suddenly blew open and exposed to the eyes of a curious public those rites and rituals reserved for the initiated only, few would understand what they saw. We must first pull back the curtain of time and peer into the temples of the ancient Mideast. Only then can we fully comprehend what transpires in the mysterious rituals and arcane ceremonies of Freemasonry.

Notes

1. Albert Mackey, *An Encyclopedia of Freemasonry* (New York: The Masonic History Company, 1915), n.p.
2. Charles Finney, *Character and Claims of Freemasonry* (Chicago: Ezra A. Cook & Co., 1879), p. 2.
3. It is interesting to note that many of the fraternal organizations of the nineteenth century eventually developed into the insurance companies of today.
4. *Scottish Rite Journal* (September 1998), p. 64.
5. James D. Shaw and Tom C. McKenney, *The Deadly Deception* (Lafayette, La.: Huntington House, 1988), p. 20. Former 33rd degree Mason Jim Shaw admits to this attraction of mystery.
6. This book was claimed to have been used as a private textbook for Masons for more than a quarter of a century.
7. Edmond Ronayne, *The Master's Carpet* (Chicago: Ezra A. Cook Publications, 1959), p. 7.

CHAPTER THREE

THE
Ancient Mysteries
Revisited

Mysteries: From the Greek word muein, to shut the mouth,
and mustes an initiate, a term for what is secret or concealed.[1]
LEWIS SPENCE, *ENCYCLOPEDIA OF OCCULTISM*

Pray also for me, that whenever I open my mouth, words may be given
me so that I will fearlessly make known the mystery of the gospel.
APOSTLE PAUL, EPHESIANS 6:19

A massive gray fortress loomed before me. I paused to pray before its broad, ascending steps that rose in sets of three, five, seven and nine. I passed between two huge sphinxlike granite lions with women's heads, poised like sentinels. Their cold, steely eyes seemed to mask Ancient Mysteries.

Towering above these guardians were 33 mammoth stone pillars, each 33 feet tall. These sacred pillars, which partially concealed an elaborate image of a sun god, created a peristyle, or colonnade, enclosing a secluded temple room within.

Once inside the great bronze doors, I entered a central court bordered by eight huge granite columns. Situated at each column was a candelabrum in the form of the god Hermes—"Bringer of Light"—an ancient Greek deity.

The lofty ceiling was marked with designs borrowed from Egyptian tombs. Adorning the chairs throughout the court were doubleheaded eagles inspired by designs on the thrones of the great Temple of Dionysus.

Statues of Isis and Nephthys, the sister-wife and sister of the Egyptian sun god, Osiris, stood nearby. I climbed the stairs to the temple room above. Directly before me was an altar of black and gold marble framed by more massive columns and walls decorated with bronze serpents.

My heart raced as I stood there, envisioning the secret ceremonies and blood oaths performed in this room on a regular basis. I shuddered as I realized how many unsuspecting men have been trapped in a deadly web of deception after visiting this eerie place.

Unfortunately, this temple scene was not a photograph torn from the pages of *Travel and Leisure*. Nor was I visiting some obscure archeological site in the Middle East. The temple is very much in use today. It is located on 16th Street in Washington, D.C., just blocks from the White House. It is the House of the Temple, the headquarters of the Supreme Council of the Southern Jurisdiction of Scottish Rite Freemasonry. It is a place full of secrets.[2]

Why would this temple house deities and icons of the mystery religions of Egypt, Greece and Rome? Surprisingly, it is to these Ancient Mysteries, with their mystic rites and sacred ceremonies, that dozens of eighteenth- and nineteenth-century Masonic historians trace the origins of Freemasonry.

The Cradle of Freemasonry

When I have quizzed Masons and ex-Masons about the history or birthplace of their Craft, more often than not I've been met with a blank stare. I am convinced that most Masons really know very little of the roots, or origins, of Freemasonry. In an article entitled "Reading Masons and Those Who Do Not Read," 33rd degree Mason Albert Mackey states:

> Nevertheless, nothing is more common than to encounter Freemasons who are in utter darkness as to everything that relates to Freemasonry. They are ignorant of its history—they do not know whether it goes back to remote ages for its origin.[3]

Why the ignorance? "They have supposed that initiation was all that was requisite to make them Masons, and that any further study was entirely unnecessary. Hence, they never read a Masonic book."[4]

If Masons would read Masonic encyclopedias and history books, what would they discover of Masonry's enigmatic origins? They would discover, as I did, that those who perpetuated their Craft could not even agree on their ancient origins. There are nearly as many opinions and theories of Masonry's roots as there are Masonic history books. Volumes have been written on when and where this secret society began.

Writers on the history of Freemasonry have at different times attributed its origin to at least a dozen sources, including:

> The Ancient Pagan Mysteries...the Temple of King Solomon...the Operative Masons of the Middle Ages...Dr. Desaguliers and his associates in the year 1717.[5]

In tracing the enigmatic origins of Masonry, we will glance at these four sources that continually resurface in Masonic literature. In showing the connection between its ancient and modern practices, I have chosen to track the stream from the mouth back to its source.

LIGHT AT THE GOOSE AND GRIDIRON

The first theory of Freemasonry's origins finds its historical roots planted at the Goose and Gridiron tavern in London, England. It was on June 24, 1717, at this tavern in St. Paul's Churchyard[6] that the Grand Lodge of England was organized. It was here that the privileges of Masonry were not limited to operative Masons, but the doors to the temples of their fraternity were thrown open to all good and true men, regardless of occupation, religion or nationality.[7] This was the beginning of speculative Masonry and was much different from the operative Masonry that preceded it. Let me explain.

My brother Alan owns a company called Campbell Masonry Construction. His company is actively involved in the craft of stonemasonry. They erect physical structures and lay blocks and brick on homes, churches and government buildings. What my brother does today is not unlike the work done by stonemasons of the Middle Ages. They traveled from site to site, erecting stone edifices. This was operative Masonry.

The second type of Masonry is speculative Masonry, another name for Freemasonry in its modern understanding. Mackey defines this type of Masonry as "the scientific application and the religious consecration of the rules and principles, the language, the implements and materials of operative Masonry to the veneration of God, the purification of the heart and the inculcation of the dogmas of a religious philosophy."[8]

In other words, you don't have to know anything about erecting buildings to be a speculative Mason (or Freemason) such as we recognize today. Presently, Freemasons simply use the symbols, secrets, ceremonies and grips of their earlier predecessors, the operative Masons.

THE MEDIEVAL BUILDING GUILDS

The second theory, common among some Masonic writers and historians proposes that Masonry's roots are deeply embedded in the soil of operative Masonry. They contend that the founding of speculative Masonry in 1717 was simply a revival of the earlier medieval operative guilds. They would concur with Mackey's words:

> Operative Masonry was...and is...the skeleton upon which was strung the living muscles and tendons and nerves of the Speculative system. It was the block of marble, rude and unpolished it may have been, from which was sculptured the life-breathing statue.[9]

As the theory goes, the skill levels of the operative masons of these builders' guilds varied greatly. A Master Mason knew considerably more than an Entered Apprentice and thus his wages were commensurate with his skill. As these masons traveled from site to site, building the gothic cathedrals, they needed a method of communicating their skill level to the foreman of the new job site. These traveling masons developed an elaborate mode of recognition involving secret signs, words, tokens and grips. According to some Masonic writers, these are the mystical roots of modern Freemasonry.

SOLOMON'S TEMPLE

A third theory is one that many current Masons accept as fact—that their origins predate even the medieval building guilds. They place the foundation of Freemasonry at the completion of Solomon's temple. This theory is based solely on the Masonic myth of Freemasonry's hero-god, Hiram Abif.[10] Masonic encyclopedist Albert Mackey, 33°, tells us:

> Time was when every Masonic writer subscribed with unhesitating faith to the theory that Masonry was there [Solomon's Temple] first organized; that there Solomon, Hiram of Tyre, and Hiram Abif presided as Grand Masters over the Lodges which they established; that there the symbolic degrees were instituted and systems of initiation were invented; and that from that period to the present Masonry has passed down the stream of Time in unbroken succession and unaltered form.[11]

Mackey then goes on record to say that "no writer who values his reputation as a critical historian would now attempt to defend this theory."[12]

THE ANCIENT MYSTERIES

Finally, the fourth theory of Freemasonry's origins is one that is commonly accepted. Masonic writers such as Robert Gould, Past Senior Grand Deacon of England, suggest that historians can't stop at the Middle Ages or Solomon's Temple to discover the origins of Freemasonry. They must continue their quest as far back as the ancient Mystery Religions of Egypt.

> I see no reason why any pause should be made in our inquiry when we reach the Middle Ages....Yet, the greater

number...of the analogies or similarities which are so much dwelt upon have their exemplars in the Mysteries to the extent that they are identical—we might with as much justice claim Egypt as the land of Masonic origin....In the Mysteries we meet with dialog, ritual, darkness, light, death and reproduction. It admits of no doubt that the rites and theological expressions of the Egyptians were of universal acceptance.[13]

Dozens of nineteenth-century Masonic scholars hold to this theory that the Masonic mysteries are deeply rooted in the Mystery religions of Egypt, Greece and Rome.

THE SACRED RITUALS AND SECRET CEREMONIES OF MODERN FREEMASONRY AND THE PAGAN MYSTERY RELIGIONS OF THE ANCIENT MIDEAST ARE MUCH TOO SIMILAR TO DENY THEIR COMMON ROOTS.

We have now moved into what Masons refer to as the realm of Masonry's legendary, nonwritten or prewritten history. Few organizations during this period kept records, and those records that were kept have since been lost or destroyed by centuries of decay. It is very important, however, not to confuse "nonwritten"

with nonexistent, nonfact or nontruth. Simply because there is little physical evidence does not prove there is no linear ascent, particularly as we deal with spiritual matters, of the Masonic mysteries from the ancient Mysteries. The sacred rituals and secret ceremonies of modern Freemasonry and the pagan Mystery Religions of the ancient Mideast are much too similar to exclude this probability. Bear with me as I try to illustrate what I mean.

The Evasive, Reemerging Serpent

As a young boy I loved to fish. After school I would grab my pole and head to Muir Springs, the local fishing hole. As I walked through the tall grass to my favorite spot, I would on occasion startle a snake that would quickly slither into the water. At first it would submerge and remain undetectable, yet all the while swimming to the center of the pond. When it determined it was at a safe distance and out of harm's way, it would emerge and slither across the top of the water.

I see the spirit that operates behind Freemasonry as not unlike the serpent at Muir Springs. This serpent, however, is much older. In fact, he is an ancient serpent. This serpent slithered into the pond of time from a shore that was possibly near the plains of Shinar in ancient Babylon. At times he was in plain view, writhing through the shadowy temples of the Mystery Religions of Mesopotamia, Egypt, Greece and Rome. He struck his victims with lightning speed, sinking his venomous fangs deep into unsuspecting victims as they bowed their hearts at the altars of pagan gods. His serpentine trail is detected in the secret ceremonies and mysterious legends, both written and oral, as they filter down through history.

At times, when this ancient serpent is startled or discovered or if it suits his best interest, he submerges. Though out of sight, he is still very much alive and on the move. At various points in history, and in diverse cultures, he reemerges. The idols, statuary and architecture of the ancients reflect his migration across Europe and Asia, tracking the power centers of the day. It is probable that he is even now coiled tightly around our own nation, the United States of America, and is devouring the destinies of our families, churches and nation.

While visible, this cunning serpent is so deceptive that few recognize him as the ancient serpent from a distant past. Cloaked in one of his latest disguises, Freemasonry, he is allowed to slither about freely even within the confines of the local church. He is still, however, a manifestation of the "god of this age" (see 2 Cor. 4:4; Eph. 2:2), spitting his venomous lies as he continues to blind the minds of unbelievers.

The Engines of Paganism

So what were the Ancient Mysteries, the religious ceremonies with secret initiations and rites? They were the engines of paganism, and they existed in most cultures of the day—in Egypt, Rome, Greece, Mesopotamia and China—and in all their worldly glory and depravity, they nurtured the pagan faith of millions of people.[14]

The peculiarities of the pagan Mysteries resembled each other to the degree that many people justifiably question if they had a common origin or ancestor. These similarities included secrecy, exoteric and esoteric rituals, a distinction between the Lesser and Greater Mysteries, degrees or levels of initiation, and they usually included the death, burial and subsequent resurrection of a hero or god.

Originally, the arcane ceremonies of the Mysteries were surrounded with the greatest secrecy and were conferred in such places as caverns or pyramids or on the highest hills in deep groves. They were practiced in honor of certain celestial or infernal gods, their secrets known to the initiates alone.

For additional secrecy, as well as impressiveness and importance, the ceremonies of the Ancient Mysteries nearly always took place at night.

The rites were practiced in the darkness of night, and often amid the gloom of impenetrable forests or subterranean caverns; and the full fruition of knowledge, for which so much labor was endured, and so much danger incurred, was not attained until the aspirant, well tried and thoroughly purified, had reached the place of wisdom and light.[15]

It was common for the initiates of the Mysteries to see displayed before their temple an image holding his finger upon his mouth to put them in mind as they went in and out of keeping secret what was done within.[16]

The Ancient Mysteries were of two kinds—the Lesser and the Greater. The Lesser Mysteries were purifactory and preparatory for the higher degrees. Some of these rituals or festivals were exoteric and were appropriate for the masses.

An initiate into these Lesser Mysteries was called a Mystes, which comes from the Greek word meaning "to shut the eyes." As a Mystes, the candidate was considered blind; but when he was initiated into the Greater Mysteries, he was called an Epopt, or "one who saw."[17] The Mystes was permitted to proceed no further than the vestibule or porch of the temple.

The Epopts alone were allowed to advance into the esoteric rituals. After they repeated the oaths that were administered to them in the Lesser Mysteries, they were ushered into the lighted sanctuary and permitted to behold in mysterious privacy what was concealed from the Mystes.[18]

For a clearer understanding of the common threads interwoven between the Mystery religions, particularly the levels of initiation and the death and resurrection of the hero-god, let's glance at the Ancient Mysteries of Egypt, Greece and Rome.

The Egyptian Mysteries

It is generally agreed that Egypt was the cradle of all the Mysteries. Philosophers of all nations went there for instructions and initiation.

> At one time in possession of all the learning and religious forms to be found in the world, [Egypt] extended into other nations the influence of its sacred rites and its Secret Doctrines.[19]

From Egypt, the Ancient Mysteries were disseminated into the civilizations of Greece, Rome and Mesopotamia. And, according to Moses Redding in his *Illustrated History of Freemasonry,* the Mysteries moved across Europe into what is now represented by the institution of Freemasonry.

> Egypt has always been considered the birthplace of the mysteries. It was there that the ceremonies of initiation were first established. It was there that the truth was first veiled in allegory, and the dogmas of religion were first imparted under symbolic forms.

This system of symbols was disseminated through Greece and Rome and other countries of Europe and Asia, giving origin, through many intermediate steps, to that mysterious association which is now represented by the institution of Free Masonry.[20]

The Egyptian Mysteries seem to have originated near the great pyramid in Memphis, though remnants of their mystic rites are found as far north as Alexandria and south to the temples of Karnak and Luxor.

From the wise men, astronomers and religious leaders of Egypt came the priesthood, and it was probably this priesthood that developed the Mysteries of Egypt.[21] It was from this priesthood that Pharaoh might have called his wise men in his infamous encounter with Moses.[22] The doctrine of these arcane Mysteries embraced cosmogony, astronomy, the arts, science, religion and the immortality of the soul. By impressive rites and ceremonies they endeavored to lead the neophyte from darkness to light, from ignorance to knowledge and a hope in the afterlife.[23]

The Egyptian Mysteries were divided into two classes—the Lesser and the Greater. While initially only the upper class or the candidates for priesthood were admitted into the Egyptian Mysteries, later they included many from the ranks of the common people. However, after the rigors of initiation, many failed to reach the Greater Mysteries.[24]

The priesthood of Egypt constituted a sacred caste, in whom the sacerdotal functions were hereditary. They exercised also an important part in the government of the state, and the kings of Egypt were but the first subjects of its priests. They had originally organized, and continued to control, the ceremonies of initiation. Their doctrines were of two kinds—exoteric or public, which were communicated to the multitude, and esoteric or secret, which were revealed to a chosen few; and to obtain them it was necessary to pass through an initiation which was characterized by the severest trials of courage and fortitude.[25]

Though little is recorded of the nocturnal rituals of the Egyptian Mysteries, it appears the candidate progressed through three degrees of initiation: The first degree was that of Isis, the second degree of Serapis and in the third degree the candidate was initiated into the rites of Osiris.

THE MYSTERIES OF ISIS

In the Mysteries of Isis the candidate was required to abstain from all unchaste acts, to restrain his appetite and to drink no wine 10 days prior to his initiation. In *Metamorphosis,* Apuleius, who had been initiated into the Mysteries in the second century A.D., speaks of the Mysteries of Isis in the following manner:

> The priest, all the profane being removed to a distance, taking hold of me by the hand, brought me into the inner recesses of the sanctuary itself, clothed in a new linen garment. I approached the confines of death and having trod on the threshold of Proserpine, I returned therefrom, being born through all the elements. At midnight I saw the sun shining with its brilliant light; and I approached the presence of the gods beneath, the gods above, and stood near and worshiped them. Behold I have related to you things of which, though heard by you, you must necessarily remain ignorant.[26]

Of his initiation into the Mysteries of Serapis and Osiris, Apuleius tells us very little, and it is therefore probable that his initiation into the Mysteries of Isis were simply preparatory to the deeper, more secretive degrees of the Greater Mysteries.

THE MYSTERIES OF SERAPIS AND OSIRIS

The Mystery of Serapis was the second degree of the Egyptian initiations. In the temple, which was built in Alexandria for the new deity and known as the Serapeum, the cult statue showed Serapis as a bearded Greek god—similar in features to Zeus— seated on a throne. It was in the subterranean caverns of this temple that the candidate took an additional solemn and binding oath of secrecy.

After due time had passed, the Adept was then raised into the Mysteries of Osiris. In the ritual of this third degree, the candidate represented Osiris and his "symbolic, mystical death and descent into the infernal regions where sin was purged away by the elements, and the initiate was said to be restored to a life of light and purity."[27]

Because the rites of Osiris are so significant, particularly as they relate to the rituals of the third degree in the mysteries of Freemasonry, it will benefit us to examine more closely the legend of this hero-god.

THE LEGEND OF OSIRIS

According to the legend, Osiris was an Egyptian king who married his sister Isis. Osiris enjoyed great popularity as a good king, which made his brother Set (or Seth) unbearably jealous. Osiris decided that a two-year trip to teach his empire about civilization, agriculture and city building was in order. During his absence he made Isis regent, and this was all it took to move Set's heart from a position of envy to that of murder. His intentions were to seize the empire and take for himself his sister Isis, after whom he lusted.

During Osiris's absence, Set made a beautiful coffin of acacia wood inlaid with silver and gold. At a banquet in honor of the 28th year of Osiris's reign, the chest was presented and offered to anyone it would fit. Well, like Cinderella's slipper, because it was custom-made, it fit only Osiris.

THE DEATH AND SEARCH FOR THE BODY

As the king slipped into the chest, Set's conspirators rushed in, nailed it shut, and flung it into the Nile. The coffin floated off to Byblos in Syria, where it came to rest in a small tamarisk or acacia tree. This tree drew the attention of the king of Byblos, who cut it down and took it to his palace, where it was then trimmed and set up as a pillar in the main hall.

Isis, also known as the goddess of a thousand names, used her magical powers to locate the coffin and went to Byblos to retrieve it. After arriving back in Egypt, she held the ankh[28] to the nose of Osiris and resurrected the body long enough to have a physical

This 2,700 year old statuette of the god Osiris was presented to the United Nations by the government of Egypt in 1976.

UN Photo 167074/ Lois Conner. Used by permission.

relationship. The next day, for whatever reason, Isis left the body unattended.

THE BURIAL

During Isis's absence, Set came upon the scene. In his anger he determined that Isis would never find the body again. He cut the body into 14 pieces, 13 of which he scattered throughout Egypt, and the 14th, Osiris's phallus, was thrown into the Nile and swallowed by a fish.

Isis, again distraught with the pain and anguish of losing her husband, sought the aid of her sister Nephthys and set out to collect the body parts. The head of Osiris she found in Abydos, and at each location where she found a part she built a shrine to the memory of her husband. Through her magical abilities she was able to retrieve all the pieces except the one eaten by the fish. With the combined effort of her sister Nephthys, Isis manufactured the organ out of wood and then again breathed life back into her dead husband.

THE RESURRECTION, OR "RAISING," OF OSIRIS

After his reconstruction, Osiris was again resurrected. However, because of the very significant piece not found, he was no longer worthy to take his place upon the throne of Egypt. Instead, Osiris was conveyed to the underworld, a dark and menacing place, where he became king and judge of the so-called dead.

Osiris, god of the Nile, was also worshiped as a fertility god. It was he who impregnated the Nile each year, effecting the inundation that caused the crops to grow. It was his symbolic death and descent into the underworld at the winter solstice that brought weeping for the wilting of the vegetation, and it was his annual resurrection in the spring that ushered in the orgiastic fertility cult festivities.

The Eleusinian Mysteries

The Eleusinian Mysteries were established in Greece about 1,800 B.C. The mythology lying behind the mysteries at Eleusis concerns Demeter, the "corn mother." In the myth, Hades entices Demeter's daughter Persephone to the underworld. In his kingdom beneath the earth, he tricks her into eating some pomegranate seeds (symbolic of marriage). No one could return from the underworld once they had eaten anything there. Zeus was asked to intervene, but he could not unconditionally demand her return to the earth. However, Persephone was permitted to dwell on earth for eight months but was required to live the remaining four below with Hades.

The Eleusinian Mysteries were the most splendid and popular of the ancient religious cults. We find in early Greek legends allusions to the sacred characteristics of these Mysteries.

The rites took place in the city of Eleusis, and their celebrations were somewhat as follows:

> In the month of September, the Eleusinian Holy Things were taken from the sacred city to Athens and placed in the Eleusinian. These probably consisted to some extent of small statues of the goddesses. Three days afterward the catechumens assembled to hearken to the exhortations of one of the priests, in which those who for any reason unworthy of initiation were solemnly warned to depart....The candidates were questioned as to their purification, and especially as regards the food they had eaten during that period. After this assembly, they betook

themselves to the seashore and bathed in the sea, being sprinkled afterwards with the blood of pigs. A sacrifice was offered up, and several days afterwards the great Eleusinian procession commenced its journey along the sacred way, its central figure being a statue of Iacchus.[29] Many shrines were visited on the way to Eleusis, where upon their arrival they celebrated a midnight orgy.[30]

The Eleusinian Mysteries were also divided into two classes—the Lesser and Greater. The Lesser were celebrated on the banks of the Illissus, and they too were intended to prepare the neophyte for his reception into the sublime rites of the Greater Mysteries.

After a period of six months, the Greater Mysteries were celebrated partly on the Thriasian plain, which surrounded the temple, and partly in the temple of Eleusis itself. It was in the initiation process in the temple that "the neophyte was then made one with the deity by partaking of holy food or drink."[31]

Much like the initiation into the Egyptian Mysteries, the process included a dramatic presentation portraying a death and resurrection. Only this time, instead of a sorrowing Isis seeking the return of Osiris from the underworld, it is a sorrowing Demeter in search of Kore (Persephone).

With the absorption of Greece into the Roman sphere of influence came a greater following, later to include a number of Roman emperors. "Cicero, himself an initiate, wrote: 'Among the many and excellent gifts of Athens to the life of mankind, none is better than those mysteries by which we are drawn from savagery into civilization.' "[32]

A number of offshoots of the Eleusinian cult were established in Greece, including the Mysteries of Dionysus and Bacchus.

The Dionysian and Bacchic Mysteries

The Roman Mysteries were commenced in honor of Bacchus, or as the Greeks called him, Dionysus. They were introduced from Egypt. In the legend, Dionysus is identified with the Egyptian Osiris.

In the ancient Mystery Religions of Greece and Rome we again find a tragedy—a murder, a search for the body, its discovery and a restoration to life.

The candidate, having been purified by water, was ushered into a vestibule and there clothed in the sacred habiliments. He was then delivered to the conductor and led through a series of dark caverns. During this march, the howling of wild beasts and artificial thunder terrified him. He remained in the darkness for three days, which commenced the mystical death of Bacchus.

As the candidate lay in the pastos, or coffin, reflecting on the nature of the undertaking in which he was engaged, he was further alarmed by more sounds. He then heard the lamentations that were instituted for the death of the god. Soon the search for the body commenced, and when it was found, the candidate was released from his confines.

The initiate was then made to descend into the infernal regions, where he beheld the torments of the wicked and the rewards of the virtuous. After this he underwent a lustration (ceremonial purification) and was ushered into the holy place, where he received the name of Epopt and was fully instructed in the doctrines of the Mysteries.[33]

It is reported that the priests of the Dionysian Mysteries devoted themselves to the study of architecture and were accorded the exclusive privilege of erecting the temples and other sacred edifices. You may recall from Scripture that Solomon conscripted the stone masons from the region of Tyre to build his temple. In all probability these masons had been initiated into the Dionysian Mysteries, and if so, these builders had an elaborate system of secret words, signs and handshakes.

In the following quote regarding the festivals and worship of Dionysus and Bacchus, one can easily recognize the similarities to the Mysteries celebrated at Eleusis:

> The leaders and the crowd that follows them perform the Bacchic dances to the accompaniment of appropriate musical instruments. These festivities are indicative of the Dionysian Dithyramb, sung to the music of the flute, and they are emblematical of the fertility of the soil. One of the emblems carried in this solemn and impressive procession is the phallus, the Bacchic symbol of reproduction. Its size is large, and it is lifted skyward by the Chief...on the sides of which ithyphallic participants are leaping in measured steps to the time of the melody of such organs as pipes, drums and flutes. Boys and girls are disguised as Satyrs, the mythological attendants of Bacchus who were sylvan deities of part man and part goat. The boys appear as Pans, the chief god of forests and pastures; the girls as nymphs and Bacchides.[34]

It's hard to imagine how gross and offensive the orgiastic festivals of the fertility cults, or ancient Mysteries, must have been. Even more difficult to imagine is why anyone would even admit that their organization sprang from such a seedbed.

There are numerous other Mystery Religions that we could discuss, including the Mithraic Mysteries, the Orphic Mysteries and the Mysteries of Adonis, to name a few. However, this will suffice to introduce the common threads of secrecy, the exoteric and esoteric rites, the levels of initiation, and the symbolic death, burial and resurrection that permeated the Mysteries of the Ancient Middle East.

If the origins of Freemasonry are deeply rooted in the soil of these Ancient Mystery religions, as Masonic scholars suggest, then I suggest that Masons and their families should begin asking some very serious questions, beginning with the question, Who is the god of the Lodge?

Notes

1. Lewis Spence, *Encyclopedia of Occultism* (New Hyde Park, N.Y: University Books, 1960), p. 281.
2. Ron Campbell, *Charisma* (November 1997), pp. 73, 74.
3. Albert G. Mackey, *Masonry Defined* (Memphis, Tenn.: Masonic Supply Co., 1925), p. 7.
4. Ibid., p. 9.
5. Mackey, *An Encyclopedia of Freemasonry,* Vol. 2 (New York: The Masonic History Company), p. 538.
6. Though the tavern has long since been destroyed, there are strong Masonic ties to St. Paul's Cathedral. On a recent private tour led by a Masonic guide, I was shown a few of the Masonic symbols in the church, including the Compass and Square and all-seeing eye painted in a quarter dome to the right of the high-altar area.
7. Moses W. Redding, *The Illustrated History of Freemasonry* (New York: Redding & Co., 1901), pp. 302, 303.
8. Mackey, *An Encyclopedia of Freemasonry,* Vol. 2, p. 704.
9. Ibid.
10. See chapter 7, subhead The Legend of Hiram Abif.
11. Mackey, *An Encyclopedia of Freemasonry,* Vol. 2, p. 769.
12. Ibid.
13. Robert Gould, quoted in Redding, *The Illustrated History of Free Masonry,* Vol. 1, p. 54.
14. John Ankerberg and John Weldon, *The Secret Teachings of the Masonic Lodge* (Chicago: Moody Press, 1990), p. 244.
15. Mackey, *An Encyclopedia of Freemasonry,* Vol. 2, p. 497.

16. William Gurnall, *The Christian in Complete Armour; A Treatise of the Saints' War Against the Devil,* originally published in 1662 (Oxford: University Press, 1983), p. 555.

17. Mackey, *An Encyclopedia of Freemasonry,* Vol. 2, p. 500.

18. Ibid.

19. R. Swineburne Clymer, M.D., *The Mysticism of Masonry* (Quakertown, Penn.: The Beverly Hall Corporation, 1993), pp. 128, 129.

20. Redding, *The Illustrated History of Freemasonry,* pp. 56, 57.

21. Ibid., p. 21.

22. See Exodus 7:11.

23. Redding, *The Illustrated History of Freemasonry,* p. 21.

24. Ibid., p. 22.

25. Ibid.

26. From the *Royal Masonic Encyclopedia,* p. 188. As quoted by Moses W. Redding, *The Illustrated History of Freemasonry* (New York: Redding & Co., 1901), p. 57.

27. Ibid., p. 25.

28. See chapter 6, subhead The Acacia Branch.

29. Iacchus appears to be Dionysus under another name.

30. Spence, *Encyclopedia of Occultism* , p. 282.

31. Ibid.

32. Norman MacKenzie, *Secret Societies* (London: Aldus Books Limited, 1967), p. 89.

33. This account of the legend of Dionysus was paraphrased from the account on pp. 213, 214 of Mackey's *An Encyclopedia of Freemasonry.*

34. J. N. Casavis, *The Greek Origin of Freemasonry* (New York: D. C. Divry, Inc., 1956), p. 159.

CHAPTER FOUR

DEMONS, MYTHS AND IDOLS

*The veneration which Masons have for the East,
confirms the theory that it is from the East that the Masonic cult
proceeded, and that this bears a relation to the primitive
religion whose first degeneration was sun worship.*[1]

BAZOT, *MASONRY DEFINED*

*He said to me, "Do you see this, son of man? You will see things that
are even more detestable than this."
He then brought me into the inner court of the house of the LORD,
and there at the entrance to the temple, between the portico and the
altar, were about twenty-five men. With their backs toward the
temple of the LORD and their faces toward the east, they were
bowing down to the sun in the east.*

GOD TO EZEKIEL, EZEKIEL 8:15,16

"We are not a secret society, but a society with secrets." It was on
my second visit to a Masonic Temple that I heard this puzzling

statement. My guide rattled it off in a monotone. Possibly he was voicing it in an attempt to present a respectable image to the outside world. I'm certain I was not the first nor the last to hear those peculiar words.

What then are the secrets of this "nonsecret society"? If they are respectable, as mentioned in the promotional brochures freely distributed by the Lodge, shouldn't they be revealed? Or if they are questionable, as many church denominations and Christian researchers have suggested, should they be concealed? Beyond what we, the "profane," are allowed to see in the exoteric activities and read in PR brochures, what really goes on behind the closed doors of the more than 13,000 Masonic Temples in the United States?

Again, most Americans assume these buildings represent a harmless fraternal organization that encourages men to help local communities. But is there more to the secret rituals of Freemasonry than meets the eye? Or more accurately, than what *doesn't* meet the eyes?

Most would be shocked to discover what many Masonic scholars and writers have revealed in books that are not easily accessible to the general public. These works hand us keys that help unlock the mysteries of Freemasonry. One such book in my library, written in the late 1800s by 33rd degree Mason Albert Pike, is entitled *Morals and Dogma of the Ancient and Accepted Scottish Rite*[2] *of Freemasonry*.[3] Printed in bold capital letters on the title page of this book is this request: "ESOTERIC BOOK, FOR SCOTTISH RITE USE ONLY; TO BE RETURNED UPON WITHDRAWAL OR DEATH OF RECIPIENT."

What is the secret sandwiched between its red covers? It confirms once again what eighteenth- and nineteenth-century Masonic scholars suggest: The roots of Freemasonry stem from a bizarre spirituality involving fertility cults and sun-god worship—forms of mythology and idolatry that have surfaced in every culture on earth and that are specifically condemned in the Bible.

Ancient Myth or Present Realities?

What is mythology? Most educated people tend to equate myth with nontruth or a story that is unbelievable. Simply stated, mythology is a collection of various legends rooted in the most ancient religious beliefs and institutions of a people. Mythology usually deals with gods and goddesses, heroes, demons and natural phenomena. Every nation has had its myths and legends, and a very close resemblance is found among them in their principal gods and heroes. The names of these mythological beings were handed down from generation to generation and passed from tribes to nations.

Mythology seems to be one of those subjects you either love or hate. You may feel as I did when I began studying this odd discipline: *Mythology, false divinities and false gods—who really cares about myth anyway? After all, aren't these false deities simply the harmless figment of man's imagination?*

These and other questions tumbled through my mind as I continued my research deep in the musty recesses of my local library. I blew the dust from one book after another and advanced my quest for knowledge.

As my research tracked the antiquated religions of the Mideast, I discovered a very important concept (I'm sure you've already discovered this, too): Our view of these ancient mythological beings as false divinities differs from those who strolled among their sculpted images and sacred pillars. Their perspective was one of worship and sacrifice, not to mythological imaginations and lifeless idols but to very present realities. The fact is, the spiritual entities that animated[4] the myths and idols of the ancients were more a reality than most of us care to imagine.

HARD-CORE IDOLATRY

Mythology and idolatry are intimately intertwined and are usually inseparable. While mythology deals with *legends* about gods and goddesses, idolatry "denotes the worship of deity in a *visible* form, whether the images to which homage is paid are symbolical representations of the true God or of the false divinities which have been made the objects of worship in his stead."[5]

The dictionary defines idolatry as "excessive devotion, or the worship of idols."[6] When most individuals in developed nations hear the word "idolatry," they think of excessive devotion or misplaced priorities involving worldly wealth. Comments I've heard, for example, include: "That man worships his new $95,000 sports car." And we've all heard comments such as, "She idolizes her new boyfriend."

While excessive devotion to anything, whether wealth, position or a person, could be viewed as idolatry, the idolatry I'm referring to is quite different. It's the blatant idolatry the prophets warned against in the Old Testament, or what C. Peter Wagner calls "hard-core" idolatry. Dr. Wagner defines idolatry as "worshiping, serving, pledging allegiance to, doing acts of obeisance to, paying homage to, forming alliances with, making covenants with, seeking power from, or in any other way exalting any supernatural being other than God."[7] Though understandably a hard pill to swallow, it is in this sense that I refer to idolatry when using it in relation to Freemasonry.

Resident Demons Behind the Myth and Idols

The apostle Paul walked and taught in the midst of pagans, those steeped in mythology and idolatry. His words to the Church in 1 Corinthians 8:4-6 and 10:19,20 are insightful:

> So then, about eating food sacrificed to idols: We know that an idol is nothing at all in the world and that there is no God but one. For even if there are so-called gods, whether in heaven or on earth (as indeed there are many "gods" and many "lords"), yet for us there is but one God, the Father....
>
> Do I mean then that a sacrifice offered to an idol is anything, or that an idol is anything? No, but the sacrifices of pagans are offered to demons, not to God, and I do not want you to be participants with demons.

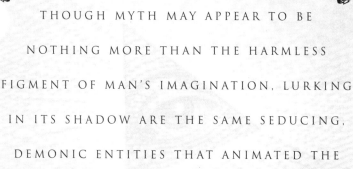

THOUGH MYTH MAY APPEAR TO BE
NOTHING MORE THAN THE HARMLESS
FIGMENT OF MAN'S IMAGINATION, LURKING
IN ITS SHADOW ARE THE SAME SEDUCING,
DEMONIC ENTITIES THAT ANIMATED THE
IDOLS OF APOSTLE PAUL'S DAY.

Do you hear what Paul is saying? Idols are nothing! However, his teaching does not stop here. A couple of chapters later Paul informs us of what is standing behind the idols—demons! The demonic realm animates that which is important to man. Though the pagans worshiped and sacrificed to idols, by whatever name or silhouette, the actual beneficiaries were demons.

Is the same concept applicable to mythology? I believe so. Though myth may appear to be nothing more than the harmless figment of man's imagination, lurking in its shadow of deception are the same seducing, demonic entities that animated the idols of Paul's day. The ultimate purpose of these dark forces is to destroy that which is precious to God.

BROTHER SUN, SISTER MOON

You may recall the rise to stardom during the late '80s of a group of characters affectionately known as the California Raisins. These cute little guys made their debut on a Hardee's restaurant commercial, depicted as plump little grapes in the process of becoming raisins. They wore fashionable sunglasses and flopped about in the sun on the deck of a swimming pool. Trendsetters of the younger generation donned T-shirts splashed with the images of these shriveled little sun worshipers. Our daughter Cassie even wore a pair of California Raisins sunglasses. I'm sure that many people can still rattle off with surprising accuracy the commercial jingle.

Unfortunately, when visiting the issue of sun worship, the blank stares of many individuals reveal their limited understanding of its serious nature. Rather, images are conjured of tanned bodies beneath Foster Grants, not unlike the little California Raisin characters simply allotting too much time to soaking up the rays at the community pool.

Worship of the solar deities is not cute, innocent, harmless or new. In fact, it's quite ancient and very deadly!

A scan of the Old Testament quickly reveals the widespread practice of bowing the heart and knees at the altars of the starry hosts. At these altars were sculpted images of the sun, moon and stars, symbols of the most prevalent forms of myth and idolatry. The sun was represented as male and viewed as the active generative principle in nature, while the moon was represented as female and seen as the passive generative principle.

Throughout the ancient Mideast, these solar deities were worshiped under many different names. To the Egyptians the sun was Osiris and the moon was his sister-wife, Isis. The Phoenicians recognized the sun as Baal, the Greeks as Apollo, the Romans as Bacchus or Dionysus, and the Mesopotamians as Tammuz.

The warnings in Scripture against yielding to the seductive spirits behind these astral deities are numerous. The book of Jeremiah, from beginning to end, is the story of a prophet weeping because of the idolatrous sins of his nation. His people were under a curse and about to be judged harshly, yet they still would not listen.

Interrupted Intercession

In the book of Jeremiah we learn that sun-god worship can actually hinder the intercession of an entire nation or people group. In Jeremiah 14 and 15, the Lord and Jeremiah were talking, and we find Jeremiah interceding on behalf of his nation. He was standing in the gap of the way things were and the way God intended them to be. He was, in a sense, the supply line, linking the need with the One who can supply. This particular case, however, was one of those situations where we've all found ourselves at one time or another. The supplier was angry and thus not willing to meet the need. In 14:11,12, the Lord said to Jeremiah,

> Do not pray for the well-being of this people. Although they fast, I will not listen to their cry; though they offer burnt offerings and grain offerings, I will not accept them.

Jeremiah's intercession was interrupted. The reason his request was denied is mentioned in Jeremiah 15:4. It is sandwiched between words of impending disaster and destruction:

> I will make [the Israelites] abhorrent to all the kingdoms of the earth because of what Manasseh son of Hezekiah king of Judah did in Jerusalem.

What did Manasseh do that was so grievous to the Lord that it interrupted intercession for an entire nation? Look in 2 Kings 21:2,3 for the answer.

> [Manasseh] did evil in the eyes of the LORD, following the detestable practices of the nations the LORD had driven out before the Israelites. He rebuilt the high places his father Hezekiah had destroyed; he also erected altars to Baal and made an Asherah pole, as Ahab king of Israel had done. He bowed down to all the starry hosts and worshiped them.

Ichabod—The Glory Departs

Ezekiel was another prophet who was keenly aware of the serious nature and consequences of idolatrous sun-god worship. While visiting with friends one afternoon, an angel of the Lord plucked him up by the hair of his head and planted him at the temple. By this act, the consternation of God's heart is clearly revealed. Something was deadly wrong and someone needed to know about it! Ezekiel was chosen, and this is what he saw:

> Then he brought me to the entrance to the north gate of the house of the LORD, and I saw women sitting there, mourning for Tammuz. He said to me, "Do you see this, son of man? You will see things that are even more detestable than this."
>
> He then brought me into the inner court of the house of the LORD, and there at the entrance to the temple, between the portico and the altar, were about twenty-five men. With their backs toward the temple of the LORD and their faces toward the east, they were bowing down to the sun in the east (Ezek. 8:14-16).[8]

Written between the lines in Ezekiel chapters 8 through 10, you will also notice the glory, the very presence of God, departing, even as Ezekiel is surveying the corrupted temple. Then, what was once a habitation of relationship is now reduced to nothing more than an institution of religion. Where once the very Spirit of life dwelt, now lingers a spirit of death and destruction. Wherever "Ichabod" is carved above the threshold of a temple (or church), it will not be coupled with the word "revival." You see, it is impossible to experience true revival without God's glory, His presence.

In this Scripture we can clearly see that the glory of the true God and the malevolent spirits operating behind the myth and idols of the sun gods, in this case Tammuz, cannot coexist. They are mutually exclusive. Idolatry will drive God far from His temple.

Numerous other Scriptures warn God's covenant people from bowing their knees to the starry hosts, including:

If a man or woman living among you in one of the towns
the LORD gives you is found doing evil in the eyes of the
LORD your God in violation of his covenant, and contrary to my command has worshiped other gods, bowing
down to them or to the sun or the moon or the stars of
the sky, and this has been brought to your attention,
then you must investigate it thoroughly (Deut. 17:2-5).

At that time, declares the LORD, the bones of the kings
and officials of Judah, the bones of the priests and the
prophets, and the bones of the people of Jerusalem will
be removed from their graves. They will be exposed to
the sun and the moon and all the stars of the heavens,
which they have loved and served and which they have
followed and consulted and worshiped (Jer. 8:1,2).

And when you look up to the sky and see the sun, the
moon and the stars—all the heavenly array—do not be
enticed into bowing down to them and worshiping
things the LORD your God has apportioned to all the
nations under heaven (Deut. 4:19).

Let's take a final glance at the tenacity, perseverance and
destructive nature of the spirits operating behind the myths and
idols of the sun gods. The scene is Mount Sinai.

Conflict on Mount Sinai

It is possible that the Israelites learned their first lessons in sun-
god worship from the Egyptians. I can still envision the scene
from the award-winning movie *The Ten Commandments*, as Moses
went up to meet with Jehovah. On this blazing mountain, God

revealed His mighty power to a trembling Moses as He struck the stone tablets with lightning, thus inscribing the Law.

However, while the true God was awing Moses on the mountain, the Israelites were engaging a false god in the valley below. In a moment of fear and doubt, they crafted an image of this sun god they carried in their hearts. This idol was the Apis bull, emblem of the procreative power of nature and symbolic of the sun god Osiris.

So all the people took off their earrings and brought them to Aaron. He took what they handed him and made it into an idol cast in the shape of a calf, fashioning it with a tool. Then they said, "These are your gods, O Israel, who brought you up out of Egypt" (Exod. 32:3,4).

What an in-your-face blasphemous irony! After all the miraculous display of God's power leveled at the gods of Egypt, culminating in the exodus from Egypt, the Israelites still lavished their praise upon a pagan deity. Unfortunately, the seducing demons behind the pagan idols didn't stop at the Red Sea, nor did they stop here at Mt. Sinai. A few centuries later this stinging phrase and blasphemous icon of the pagan fertility cults reappeared in northern Israel.

In direct disobedience to God's commands, King Solomon embraced the idols of his foreign wives, so God divided his kingdom. Jeroboam soon became king of the northern kingdom, while Rehoboam ruled in the south. Compelled by fear of losing his kingship to Rehoboam, Jeroboam crafted two golden calves. After positioning these fertility deities near Bethel and Dan, he echoed the blasphemous words Aaron had voiced in the valley near Mount Sinai: "Here are your gods, O Israel, who brought you up out of Egypt" (1 Kings 12:28).

To this day, vestiges of pagan worship exist within ancient archeological sites, revealing the former existence of temples, tombs and sacred pillars—all evidence of abandonment of worship of the one true God.

Notes

1. Albert Mackey, *Masonry Defined* (Memphis, Tenn.: Masonic Supply Co., 1925), p. 106.
2. Ancient and Accepted (Scottish) Rite: A system of thirty-three degrees developed out of the eighteenth-century French Rite of Perfection of twenty-five degrees. Outside the British Isles it is referred to as the Scottish Rite, many of the original French degrees having *Ecossais* in their titles. In Britain it is a Christian Order, but in most other countries it is as universalist as the Craft.
3. Henry Leonard Stillson, editor in chief, *History of the Ancient and Honorable Fraternity of Free and Accepted Masons* (London: The Fraternity Publishing Company, 1921), p. 54.
4. Animated means "to enliven."
5. Wm. Smith LL.D., *Bible Dictionary* (Philadelphia, Penn.: The John C. Smith Company, 1884), p. 262.
6. Ibid., pp. 250, 251.
7. Peter Wagner, *Hard-Core Idolatry, Facing the Facts* (Colorado Springs: Wagner Institute for Practical Ministries, 1999), p. 11.
8. The women of Jerusalem were bewailing his (Tammuz's) dying, which they felt caused the annual wilting of vegetation. *The NIV Study Bible* (Grand Rapids, Mich: Zondervan Publishing House, 1985).

CHAPTER FIVE

TEMPLES, TOMBS AND SACRED PILLARS

The Grand Lodge of New York laid the cornerstone for "Cleopatra's Needle" in New York City's Central Park on October 9, 1880, before 30,000 spectators.[1]

S. BRENT MORRIS, *CORNERSTONES OF FREEDOM*

There in the temple of the sun in Egypt he will demolish the sacred pillars and will burn down the temples of the gods of Egypt.

JEREMIAH 43:13

As we entered the port city of Alexandria, Egypt, the variant speeds of carts, motor scooters, buses and taxis heightened the trepidation of navigating its narrow, overcrowded streets. Fortunately, Mohammed, our Egyptian taxi driver, was familiar with the transit peculiarities of this metropolis. Darla and I, along with our good friend Rick Ridings, soon stepped out of the cab at our final destination.

We walked up a rocky hill to where the ancient Temple of Serapis once stood and saw a mammoth granite pillar rising 88 feet into the sky. While it once adorned the sacred temple and beckoned votaries of the Osiris-Serapis cult, it now serves as a silent sentinel at the doorway to Egypt's past. In all probability, the paths we strolled were tread by the likes of Cleopatra, Marc Antony and Trajan.

After visually surveying and praying the perimeters of this sacred promontory with its sphinx and column fragments, we made our way down to the subterranean Serapeum.[2] There we observed two chambers. Both were locked. I looked through the iron gate into the first chamber and found it to be nothing more than a small vaulted sepulcher. A placard informed us that in this chamber a sacred Apis[3] bull had been discovered. We peered through the gates of the second chamber and were about to leave when the caretaker met us with the key. Though he insisted that we enter this hallowed cavern, he didn't lead or even follow us in.

The air inside the Serapeum was damp and musty. An eerie darkness seemed to enfold us as we descended the gentle incline deeper into the cavern. The walls of this consecrated corridor were pockmarked with niches in which the faithful Egyptians had placed tablets or possibly small stelae in honor of the bulls. I couldn't help wondering what had really transpired in these subterranean chambers under this ancient Temple of Serapis. The deeper we hiked, the more claustrophobic I felt and the more intense our prayers.

After several minutes, we heard our Arabic escort calling us from the mouth of the cavern. It was time to go. This was one of those visits when you say, "Been there, done that, not sure it needs repeating!"

In a few moments we were back in the sunlight and positioned near the sacred pillar. It was time for reflection, declaration of the Word and more prayer.

GONE WITH THE WIND?

Most of the temples, tombs and sacred pillars of Osiris, Isis and Serapis have crumbled into the distant past. Not much physical evidence remains, so one must rely heavily on ancient writ and active imagination to envision the sacred activity on this hilltop nearly 3,000 years ago.

But is it really all gone? If we refer to the collective stones cemented into the physical edifice, then yes, they are gone. I stood on the rubble of what may have been a roof, column, portico, sacred bath or maybe even an altar. They were now nothing more than pebbles beneath my dusty feet.

But what about the mysterious rites and sacred ceremonies performed in these subterranean caverns by the god-kings and high priests, the sages and adepts? And what of the exoteric rituals of the common people who bowed at the sacred altars of this religious high place? Were they blown into history by the winds of time? I don't think so!

AS NATIONS ROSE AND FELL, THE GODS OF THE ANCIENT MYSTERY RELIGIONS SIMPLY CLOAKED THEMSELVES IN THE RELIGIOUS ICON OF THE LATEST CULTURE AND MIGRATED THROUGH HISTORY TO A NEW LOCUS OF POWER.

It is quite probable that the secret rituals and ceremonies enacted on the highest hills and in the lowest caverns of ancient Egypt yet remain. As the winds of adversity blew and nations rose and fell, the gods of these ancient Mystery religions simply cloaked themselves in the religious icon of the latest culture and migrated through history to a new locus of power. They still demand worship and devotion from their latest votaries.

Solar Shrines

The solar shrines of the old solar religion, like the Masonic Temples, were usually oriented on an east-west axis. This was purposely done "so that on one day of the year the beams of the rising sun, or of some bright star that hailed his coming, should stream down the nave and illumine the altar."[4] These solar shrines were of the same essential plan:

> A large forecourt with cultus chambers on each side, and a huge altar; while in the rear, rising from a mastaba-like base was a tall obelisk.[5]

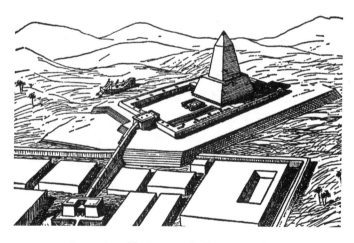

Restoration of the Sun-Temple of Nuserre at Abusir.
A History of Egypt by James Henry Breasted, Ph.D.
(New York: Charles Scribner's Sons), 104. Used by permission.

This was the symbol of the god, standing exposed to the sky, and there was therefore no Holy of Holies. There are reasons for supposing that the obelisk and connected portions of the building were but an enlargement of the Holy of Holies in the temple at Heliopolis.[6]

Sphinx, House of the Temple, Washington, D.C.
Photo by author.

A visit to many Masonic Lodges may impress you as a visit to Egypt itself. Sphinxlike creatures flank the portals of many Lodges, such as the House of the Temple in Washington, D.C. In addition, many of the Lodges I have visited, including the Grand Lodges of Colorado and Pennsylvania, house elaborate Egyptian rooms, which include numerous images of the solar deities.

The most evocative symbol of Freemasonry's obsession with Egypt is not hidden behind the Lodge doors but is openly displayed in many of the major cities of the world. It is the obelisk—the symbol of the procreative power of the sun gods.

Romancing the Sacred Stones

Jeremiah refers to obelisks in Jeremiah 43:13. Heliopolis, the "city of the sun" was a center for sun-god worship and was recognized for these sacred pillars. What is an obelisk? You've probably seen them and may not have known what they represented. An obelisk is a "quadrangular, monolithic column, diminishing upward, with the sides gently inclined, but not so as to terminate in a pointed apex, but to form at the top a flattish pyramidal figure, by which the whole is finished off and brought to a point."[7]

The easiest way I could teach you what an obelisk looks like is to direct your attention to the center of the cross axis of the federal district of the United States, in Washington, D.C. There you will see the Washington Monument, a 555-foot reproduction of the original obelisks of Egypt.

The obelisks of the solar temples provided a focal point; they were cult symbols of the sun god. They were and still are idols. In predynastic times they were worshiped as miraculous shafts of stone on which the sun was thought to rest upon its rising.

The spirit of the Sun-god was supposed to enter the stones at certain periods, and on these occasions human sacrifices were offered to it. The victims were probably prisoners of war who had been captured alive, and foreigners, and when these failed, the priests must have drawn upon the native population.

At On-Heliopolis, king after king erected benbens in Re's honor, so that by 1,300 B.C. the city was full of obelisks: some decorated with gold to resemble the sun's rays, others with inscriptions glorifying Re's daily passage through the skies, or hailing earthly occasions such as victories, feasts and jubilees.

The United States acquired an obelisk in 1881, when "Cleopatra's Needle," a gift of the khedive, was erected in New York's Central Park. Once it stood before the Temple of the Sun at Heliopolis.

Photographer Unknown/NGS Image Collection.
Used by permission.

The pharaohs of later dynasties switched their obelisk-erecting affections to Osiris: God of the earth, vegetation and the Nile flood that gave life to all Egypt; God of rebirth; God also of the Underworld, the Last Judgment and Life after Death.[8]

Today, fewer than a dozen obelisks remain standing in Egypt. Many have been moved to other parts of the world, including two of them to Nineveh and many to Rome, Constantinople, Paris and London. One of these sacred pillars was even floated to Central Park in New York City and dedicated by the Masons upon its arrival. Supposedly there are over 50 obelisks in public squares and parks throughout Europe and North America.

My wife and I, along with teams of intercessors, have visited many of these sacred pillars. As I stood in their shadows in Paris and New York City and on the banks of the Thames River in London, I couldn't help but wonder what was on the heart of God regarding these ominous monoliths. If idolatry ushers in consequential judgment and curses, is it possible that we have opened the door to something less than God's best for our cities and nations? What were we thinking, or more accurately *were* we thinking, when we allowed these obelisks to be positioned on our public squares? Personally, I sense no compromise in the heart of God regarding these sacred pillars. In fact, a quick perusal of the Old Testament would indicate quite the contrary, as evidenced by the word spoken in Jeremiah 43:13:

> There in the temple of the sun in Egypt he will demolish the sacred pillars[9] and will burn down the temples of the gods of Egypt.

In the Lowest Valleys

It was common among the ancients to practice their idolatrous worship on the highest hills and lowest valleys, usually in sacred groves or subterranean caverns. Worshiping on the highest hills and in the lowest valleys served a dual purpose. It not only provided the necessary protection and privacy, but it also positioned the aspirants closer to the celestial deities (sun, moon and stars) and the infernal, or terrestrial, deities.[10]

On a recent trip to Jerusalem I led a small brigade of prayer warriors into a subterranean cavern. I clutched a copy of a 130-year-old map as we stumbled down the dimly lit main corridor while a labyrinth of smaller rooms opened in every direction. The smell of the damp, musty air was reminiscent of a childhood float through the watery cave of "It's a Small World" at Disneyland. The stone chips under our feet and the lamp niches carved into the walls with their still-visible streaks of soot were the only vestiges of activity in this cave from nearly 3,000 years ago. The oil lamps that once illumined the sweat-drenched backs of laborers in this ancient workplace had also cast upon its walls the dancing shadows of other, more arcane activities.

It was my quest for truth and understanding of these secret rituals that enticed me halfway around the world. My unwavering desire to view with my own eyes the reality of what was etched on my antiquated map lured me into this significant subterranean cavern—Solomon's Quarries under the old city of Jerusalem.

CAVERNS OF MYSTERY

It was here in Solomon's Quarries, according to a legend taught by Dr. Robert Morris, that the ancients, led by Solomon, engaged in the secret rituals of the Mysteries.[11]

> At the extreme end of the quarry is a basin cut in the rock for holding water. Here stood King Solomon during the ceremony I am about to describe; upon his right

hand King Hiram, upon his left Adoniram; before him, group upon group, the Builders of the Temple....King Solomon took water from the basin in his right hand, threw it seven times around and before him, and prayed thus to the King of kings: "May the blessing of God, supremely good and great, descend upon us, genial and free as the dew of Herman on a summer night. May the sweet influences of brotherly love be diffused over our souls and make them perpetually green. May this covenant of blood into which we are about to enter keep us true and faithful unto death." And the great multitude bowed and murmured amen. So mote [sic] it be! The esoteric proceeding followed.[12]

THE MOOT LODGE

I had come to this cavern to investigate not only the facts and fiction of three millennia gone by, but also the rumors of more recent arcane rituals performed on the site where I now stood in the bowels of the earth and out of sight of the public eye.

Masonic history records that this mysterious cavern is associated with the oldest traditions of Freemasonry. It was here, states Dr. Morris in his book *Freemasonry in the Holy Land*, that a moot Lodge (the meeting was considered moot, or disputable, because the Lodge meeting was not properly chartered) was held in 1868, "to introduce Freemasonry, though cautiously and judiciously, into the Holy Land."[13]

Entering with a good supply of candles, we pushed southward as far into the quarry as we could penetrate and found a chamber happily adapted to a Masonic purpose. It was a pit in the ancient cuttings, about eighteen feet square. On the east and west, convenient shelves had been left by the original workmen, which answered for seats. An upright stone in the center, long used by guides to set their candles upon, served us for an altar. About ten feet above the master's station there was an immense opening in the wall, which led, for aught I know, to the original site of the temple of Solomon. We were perfectly tiled by silence, secrecy and darkness, and in the awful depths of that quarry, nearly a quarter of a mile from its opening, we felt, as we never had before, how impressive is a place which none but the All-seeing Eye can penetrate.[14]

Our prayer group pursued the echo of trickling water to the end of the cave and located the water basin mentioned by Dr. Morris. I also observed what appeared to be seats or makeshift thrones carved into the stone and I nearly stumbled into a pit where a skeleton had been discovered earlier. I found that nearly all the physical surroundings yet remained as described by Dr. Morris.

As we tracked the dotted lines on my map that led us to our final destination in this man-made labyrinth, spiritual darkness seemed to engulf our already dim surroundings. While King Solomon's mysterious activity in this cavern is possible,[15] it is not provable. It is certain, however, that 130 years ago, on the very spot where I now stood, secret rituals were performed by Freemasons. Directly before me on a dimly lit plaque was the name of this carved-out subterranean cathedral, "Freemason's Hall." You see, to this day secret Masonic rituals are conducted here annually, attended by Masons from around the globe!

The annual mysterious rites in Solomon's Quarries are not isolated incidents. It may surprise you to know that Masons continue to open their Lodges on the highest hills and in the lowest valleys, not just symbolically, but often physically as well.

Amongst other observances which were common to both the true and spurious Freemasonry, we find the practice of performing commemorative rites *on the highest of hills and the lowest of valleys*. This practice was in highest esteem amongst all the inhabitants of the ancient world, from a fixed persuasion that the summit of mountains made a nearer approach to the celestial deities, and the valley, or holy cavern to the infernal and submarine gods than the level country; and therefore, the prayers of mortals were more likely to be heard in such situations.[16]

DEATH VALLEY, THE LOWEST VALE

Six thousand miles from Jerusalem, at a site 10 miles southwest of Furnace Creek Inn in the heart of Death Valley, California, a special meeting of Winnedumah Lodge No. 287 was held on April 10, 1937. W. A. Chalfant, member of the Grand Lodge Committee on Masonic History, provides the following account:

> Our ancient Brethren who held their meeting on the mountaintops have been emulated more than once by modern Lodges. It remained for the Lodges of the 60th Masonic District embracing the Lodges of Mono and Inyo Counties of California to more than rival those of long ago in the selection of the lowest vale for their place of meeting. They have set a mark in that respect which has never been equaled on this continent, or probably anywhere else in the world.[17]

The occasion worthy of becoming historic was on the floor of Death Valley at a point 270 feet below sea level, 10 feet above bad water. "A dry lake bed of tablelike smoothness, the lowest spot on the continent, offered a satisfactory site."[18]

On the Highest Hills

THE SENTINEL DOME ALTAR

On August 14, 1937, the members of Mariposa Lodge No. 24 opened a lodge on the summit of Sentinel Dome, a rounding granite mountaintop in Yosemite National Park that is 8,117 feet above sea level. The top of the dome, being nearly flat, had been carefully prepared by the brethren in advance of the ceremony. They had built up a stone altar and stone pedestals.[19]

> [It was] a night when the cloudless canopy of a star-decked heaven truly formed a covering of the lodge and where, in fact, our modern brethren met on one of the highest hills.[20]

In addition to erecting an altar on Sentinel Dome in Yosemite, three years later and 200 feet higher, the Masons chose Mount Abel as a site to "raise" a candidate to the degree of Master Mason.

THE MASTERS ON MOUNT ABEL

On August 17, 1940, the Masons of Kern County, California, conferred the Master Mason degree upon a candidate in a natural amphitheater surrounded by towering pillars of pine and fir on the summit of Mt. Abel, 8,300 feet above sea level.[21] It was considered a high point in California Freemasonry (no pun intended).

> The lodge room consisted of all out of doors, under the canopy of Heaven lighted by a summer moon. Beautiful

trees formed a background for the natural stage. The
"Lodge Room" was properly tiled.[22]

Sleeping with the Enemy

The Old Testament prophets more than suggest that engaging
in idolatry on the highest hills actually involved entering into
pacts with pagan deities. It was spiritual adultery. Isaiah calls
our attention to these abominable practices:

> You have made your bed on a high and lofty hill; there
> you went up to offer your sacrifices. Behind your doors
> and your doorposts you have put your pagan symbols.
> Forsaking me, you uncovered your bed, you climbed into
> it and opened it wide; you made a pact with those whose
> beds you love, and you looked on their nakedness. You
> went to Molech with olive oil and increased your per-
> fumes. You sent your [idols] far away; you descended to
> the grave itself! (Isa. 57:7-9).

Other peculiar places where Masons have opened their
lodges include inactive volcanoes and abandoned gold mines.
These examples were lifted from the pages of the history of the
Grand Lodge of California. I'm certain that further research of
the Grand Lodges of other states would reveal odd meetings in
mysterious places as well, again on the highest hills and in the
lowest valleys.

Finally, with an understanding of the idolatrous worship of
the solar deities of the Ancient Mysteries, let us now look behind
the "tiled" doors of the Masonic Lodge, beginning with a journey through Freemasonry symbol.

Notes

1. S. Brent Morris, *Cornerstones of Freedom* (Washington, D.C.: The Supreme Council, 33°, S.J., 1993), p. 126.
2. A subterranean structure where the sacred Apis bulls were buried.
3. From this bull we get the name Ser*apis*.
4. Joseph Newton, *The Builders: A Story and Study of Freemasonry* (New York: Macoy Publishers and Masonic Supply Co., 1951), p. 11.
5. Albert Mackey, *An Encyclopedia of Freemasonry* (New York: The Masonic History Company, 1915), p. 525.
6. James Henry Breasted, *A History of Egypt* (New York: Charles Scribner's Sons, 1905), p. 105.
7. Mackey, *An Encyclopedia of Freemasonry*, p. 525.
8. Martin Short, *Inside the Brotherhood* (New York: Dorset Press, 1989), pp. 81, 82.
9. Jeremiah 43:13 footnote, *Sacred Pillars*. Obelisks, for which ancient Heliopolis was famous, *The NIV Study Bible* (Grand Rapids, Mich.: Zondervan Publishing House, 1985).
10. Albert Mackey, *Masonry Defined* (Memphis, Tenn.: Masonic Supply Co., 1925), p. 154.
11. Robert Morris, *Freemasonry in the Holy Land* (New York: Masonic Publishing Company, 1875), n.p.
12. Rev. Henry R. Coleman, *Light from the East* (Louisville, Ky.: Knight & Leonard, 1881), p. 470.
13. Morris, *Freemasonry in the Holy Land*, p. 465.
14. Ibid., p. 463.
15. First, Solomon may have been introduced to the nocturnal rituals of the Mysteries during the construction of his temple. "Over this construction, Hiram (not to be confused with the Masonic hero, Hiram Abif), the craftsman of Tyre, presided. At Tyre the Mysteries of Bacchus had been introduced by the Dionysian Artificers (those workers initiated into the Mysteries of Dionysus), and into their fraternity, Hiram, in all probability, had been admitted." Secondly, 1 Kings 11 is the sad commentary of King Solomon being led astray through disobedience and idolatry. Contrary to God's commands, he married foreign women who turned his heart after other gods. He followed Ashtoreth, the goddess of the Sidonians, and Molech, the detestable god of the Ammonites. The hill east of Jerusalem is still a silent witness to the abominable acts of worship and child sacrifice to these foreign deities. A great man of tremendous anointing bowed his knee at the altar of pagan gods.
16. Albert Mackey, *Masonry Defined*, p. 325.
17. Leon O. Whitsell, Past Grand Master, *One Hundred Years of Freemasonry in California* (San Francisco: Grand Lodge, Free and Accepted Masons of California, 1950), p. 321.

18. Ibid., pp. 322, 323.
19. Ibid., p. 325.
20. Ibid., p. 327.
21. Ibid.
22. Ibid.

CHAPTER SIX

A JOURNEY THROUGH FREEMASONRY SYMBOL

Masonry, successor of the Mysteries, still follows the ancient manner of teaching. Her ceremonies are like the ancient mystic shows—not the reading of an essay, but the opening of a problem, requiring research, and constituting philosophy the arch-expounder. Her symbols are the instruction she gives. The lectures are endeavors, often partial and one-sided, to interpret these symbols.[1]

ALBERT PIKE
*MORALS AND DOGMA OF THE ANCIENT AND ACCEPTED
SCOTTISH RITE OF FREEMASONRY*

Although I am less than the least of all God's people, this grace was given me: to preach to the Gentiles the unsearchable riches of Christ, and to make plain to everyone the administration of this mystery,[2] which for ages past was kept hidden in God, who created all things.

APOSTLE PAUL, EPHESIANS 3:8,9

Pagan Symbols in a Sacred Grove

One evening in the fall of 1996, I had occasion to see an exceptionally high concentration of pagan symbols in a sacred grove in Colorado. I had heard about a pagan new-moon festival near Colorado Springs, so I mentioned to a friend my interest in interviewing these folks. We decided to sneak up on their coven and observe from a distance their unusual rituals before moving in for the possible interview. Because we didn't know the exact location and because these pagan worshipers were not visible from a distance, our approach was not exactly under cover. Needless to say, they discovered us before we located them.

We broke through the trees and into a clearing not 30 feet from where the witches were seated. Fortunately for us, they were civil. As they waited for their high priest to arrive, they consented to answer my questions. Upon his arrival, the high priest even invited us to stay and observe as they engaged in their sacred rituals.

As they "cut the circle," lit the candles and invoked the spirits of the four cardinal points, the sounds and sights were eerie. Entire families danced in the circle, including children of all ages. The majority of those participating in the festival were clothed in black, and all had a symbol of their religion dangling from their neck and ears, which was the pentagram, or inverted five-pointed star. Even the children sported their own personal icon of this pagan religion. It was obvious that this symbol evoked a spiritual emotion and greatly played into their identity.

A symbol can be defined as a visible sign with which a spiritual feeling, emotion or idea is connected.[3] We are surrounded by symbols. If you drive past a Christian church, you might see a religious symbol in the form of a cross. Some Christians display the symbol of the fish on the rear bumpers of their cars.

The crescent moon is a symbol of Islam. While researching in

Egypt during the fall of 1998, I observed the crescent moon atop dozens of mosques and minarets silhouetted against the skyline. If you have an interest in Israel, you may wear a pendant of the Star of David or the Menorah, symbols of this predominantly Jewish nation.

Symbols: Modes of Instruction and Communication

In addition to evoking religious emotions, symbols have been used as modes of communication and instruction for millennia. It is suggested that when language was in its infancy, visible symbols were the most vivid means of acting upon the minds of hearers.[4] The ancient Egyptians communicated through the use of hieroglyphics, which were pictures, or symbols. A quick perusal of any Egyptian tour book will reveal the ancients' ability to symbolically portray their messages on their temples, tombs and sacred pillars. Most languages today, including our own English language, are still comprised of letters that are nothing less than symbols.

Symbols communicate a message. For example, when you see a yield sign, you know what it means even if you can't read the word "yield." Likewise, when you see the skull and crossbones on an amber bottle, you immediately recognize its contents as harmful. If this odd symbol is displayed on a fence or enclosure, it immediately communicates a sense of danger.

Symbols and Freemasonry

Masons today still use strange symbols, including the mysterious skull and crossbones. In fact, all the instructions in Freemasonry's mysteries are communicated in the form of symbols.[5] These symbols help us to identify what Masonry is and provide us with possible keys to this organization's ancient past. "The Square and Compass is the most widely used and known symbol of Masonry. In one way, this symbol is a kind of trademark for the fraternity, as the golden arches are for McDonald's."[6] The symbols of the first three degrees of Freemasonry are drawn from the medieval stonemasons' guilds, the profession which it "spiritualizes."[7] The Grand Lodges claim that they are simply the custodians of these ancient symbols; that is, they protect them from change yet do not seek to interpret them.

> The interpretation of the symbols, if it is to be done at all, is the responsibility of the individual Mason; and it is in the process of that personal interpretation—and of seeing the principles that emerge operate in one's own life—that one can see the Craft of Freemasonry come alive as a "Mystery."[8]

I'VE FOUND THE INTERPRETATIONS OF

MASONIC SYMBOLS TO BE MULTILEVEL

AND VERY DISTURBING WHEN EXPOSED

TO THE LIGHT OF SCRIPTURE.

Although the Masonic Lodge gives the impression that it does not interpret the symbols for the candidate, there is no lack of printed material by Masonic writers on the subject of Masonic symbolism. I've found the interpretations of these bizarre symbols to be multilevel and, quite frankly, very disturbing when exposed to the light of Scripture.

Stratum Theory of Masonic Symbolism

You won't find stratum theory listed in Mackey's *Encyclopedia of Freemasonry,* yet it is written on nearly every page of that aged book. Masonic symbols have several layers, or stratum. An attempt to examine these symbols is not unlike peeling an onion. After you have examined one layer, you discover that it's merely the protective covering of a deeper, more arcane concept or teaching. Many church leaders and researchers, including myself, who have labored endless hours researching the deeper interpretations and explanations of the symbols of Masonry have been accused by Masons of exercising overactive imaginations. It matters not to them that our conclusions were formed *after* studying Masonic sources.

I have identified at least three layers of interpretation of Masonic symbols. First are the interpretations for the profane, or non-Masons. As mentioned in chapter 1, I believe these interpretations are fashioned to keep the curious public at bay. The second level includes deeper yet seemingly harmless interpretations taught to the candidates of the lower degrees. They do not explain enough to shake the candidate from the seduction of Masonry's curious mysteries.

Deeper yet is the third level of interpretation of Masonic symbols. They are reserved for the elect. We find this confession of Masonic scholar Albert Pike:

> Masonry, like all the religions, all the Mysteries, Hermeticism and alchemy, conceals its secrets from all

except the Adepts and Sages, or the Elect, and uses false explanations and misinterpretations of its symbols to mislead those who deserve only to be misled; to conceal the truth, which it calls light, from them, and to draw them away from it. Truth is not for those who are unworthy or unable to receive it, or would pervert it.[9]

Did you get that? Pike informs us that candidates are intentionally misled by false explanations of Masonic symbols! This explains why getting to the truth of Freemasonry is so difficult. Interspersed with bits of the real truth is another truth that Masonry calls "light." It is great deception. At what level does deception end and truth begin? Who, then, is an Adept worthy of "truth?" Mackey informs us that an Adept is:

One that is fully skilled or well versed in any art; from the Latin word "adeptus," *having obtained*, because the Adept claimed to be in the possession of all the secrets of his peculiar mystery....In the similar allusion to the possession of abstruse knowledge, the word is applied to some of the high degrees of Masonry.[10]

It is this deeper level, the realm of Adepts, Sages and the Elect, that is the most confusing. Why? Because someone appears to be calling truth deception and deception truth. Or more accurately, light is called dark and dark light!

The Tracing Boards

In the early days of speculative Freemasonry, the work of the Lodge consisted mainly of lectures. The symbols that illustrated the lectures were sketched on the Lodge floor. To maintain secrecy after every teaching, the symbols were erased from the floor. This laborious process was replaced during the eighteenth century by floor cloths painted with the principal symbols. Later, these were replaced by the smaller, more durable tracing boards.[11] Although there is a tracing board for most degrees in Masonry, we will only look at the boards of the first three degrees.

THE FIRST-DEGREE TRACING BOARD

The tracing board of the Entered Apprentice is an integrated picture used to illustrate the principles of the first degree. Because the symbols on this board are numerous, we will examine only the major ones.

THE TESSELLATED BORDER

As the initiate steps into the realm of Masonic mysteries, the first symbol he should notice is the tessellated border. It is the cord that surrounds the tracing board and is decorated with tassels at the four corners. Mackey's encyclopedia renders this explanation of the border:

> The tracing-board being a representation of the lodge, and [the tessellated border] symbolizes the bond of love—*the mystic tie*—which binds the Craft wheresoever dispersed into one band of brotherhood[12] (italics mine).

This sounds rather harmless, doesn't it? However, as is the case with many of Masonry's unusual symbols, in order to ferret out a clear understanding you must look up the definitions of the words within the definition. For example, what does Mackey mean by the "Mystic Tie" with which the Mason is bound? On another page of the same encyclopedia, it is defined as:

First Degree Tracing Board

From *Freemasonry: A Journey Through Ritual and Symbol* by W. Kirk MacNulty,
published by Thames and Hudson Inc., New York.
Copyright, and reproduced by permission, of the United Grand Lodge of England.

That sacred and inviolable bond that unites men of the
most discordant opinions into one band of brothers,
which gives but one language to men of all nations and

one altar to men of all religions, is properly, from the mysterious influence it exerts, denominated the mystic tie; and Freemasons, because they alone are under its influence, or enjoy its benefits, are called "Brethren of the mystic tie"[13] (italics mine).

While it is true that we live, move and have our being on an earth populated primarily with unbelievers, it is more than a little disconcerting when we bow at a common altar. In fact, Scripture clearly warns against it: "Do not be yoked together with unbelievers."[14]

THE CHECKERED PAVEMENT

Once we have entered this mystical realm of Freemasonry, our feet are planted on a checkered, or mosaic, pavement. This pavement is always preserved as an ornament of the Lodge, seen particularly on the tracing boards of the first three degrees. "By a *little torsion* of historical accuracy, the Masons have asserted that the ground floor of the Temple was a mosaic pavement, and hence as the Lodge is a representation of the Temple, that the floor of the Lodge should also be of the same pattern"[15] (italics mine).

These checkered pavements were common in the temples of the ancients; the Egyptians, the Greeks and especially the Romans ingeniously decorated the floors of their temples in this manner.[16]

Albert Pike states that "the pavement, alternately black and white, symbolizes, intended or not, the good and evil principles of the Egyptian and Persian creed."[17]

THE TRESTLE BOARD

The trestle boards are not to be confused with the tracing boards. While all degrees have a tracing board, only the Entered Apprentice degree has a trestle board. The trestle boards of the ancient building guilds could be compared to today's architectural blueprints.

> In the Masonic ritual, the Speculative Mason is reminded that, as the Operative artist erects his temporal building in accordance with the rules and designs laid down on the trestle board of the master workman, so should he erect that spiritual building, of which the material is a type, in obedience to the rules and designs, the precepts and commands laid down by the Great Architect of the Universe [GAOTU] in those great books of nature and revelation which constitute the spiritual trestle board of every Freemason.[18]

I believe that the GAOTU as represented by Freemasonry is not the God of Abraham, Isaac and Jacob. He is not the God of the New Testament. Mackey informs us that the origins of Freemasonry are different. He further states:

> If Masonry were simply a Christian institution, the Jews and the Moslem, the Brahman and the Buddhist could not conscientiously partake of its illumination. But its universality is its boast. In its language citizens of every language may converse; at its altar men of all religions may kneel; to its creed disciples of every faith may subscribe.[19]

This seems to contradict Jesus, who said, "I am the way and the truth and the life. No one comes to the Father except through me" (John 14:6).

So who is this mysterious god of the Lodge? A man should be able to easily see how deadly it would be to submit the design and development of his "spiritual temple" to a universal god at whose altars men of all religions bow!

THE ROUGH AND SMOOTH ASHLARS

The candidate is represented by the rough ashlar, a building stone that has not yet been shaped into the form required by its place in the structure.

Freemasonry regards humanity as a "Temple of God. The obvious implication—that the candidate is expected to use the experiences of his own life *to work on himself and to make himself* a stone properly 'shaped' to take his own unique place in that temple—is exactly the one that is intended"[20] (italics mine).

When Masonic education has exerted its influence in expanding the candidate's intellect, restraining his passions and purifying his life, he is then represented by the smooth, or perfect, ashlar, which, under the skillful hand of the workmen, is placed in the temple.[21]

The very important question we must ask is, Whose temple is the initiate being shaped for and cemented into? I'm convinced that it isn't the temple Peter speaks of in 1 Peter 2:5.

THE POINT WITHIN A CIRCLE BETWEEN TWO PARALLEL LINES

Just below the ladder you will see a point within a circle between two parallel lines. These bizarre symbols provide a case in point for our "stratum theory" of interpretation. What the candidate is told in the first degree is just a portion of the bigger picture. He deals first with the moral and political meaning of the symbols, while their philosophical and spiritual import are reserved for later.

In the first degree, the candidate is asked to whom the Lodge is dedicated. His memorized and coached answer:

> To St. John the Baptist and St. John the Evangelist, who were two eminent Christian patrons of Masonry; and since their time there is, or ought to be, represented in

every regular and well-governed Lodge, a certain *"point within a circle,"* the point representing an individual brother, the circle the boundary-line of his conduct beyond which he is never to suffer his prejudices or passions to betray him. This circle is embodied by two perpendicular parallel lines, representing St. John the Baptist and St. John the Evangelist; and upon the top rests the Holy Scriptures. In going round this circle we necessarily touch upon these two lines[22] (italics mine).

First, let me assure you that John the Baptist and John the Evangelist were not patrons of Freemasonry. Masonic sources even admit this fact.

We are thus led to the conclusion that the connection of the Saints John with the Masonic Institution is rather of a symbolic than of an historical character.[23]

Masonic encyclopedist Albert Mackey, 33°, informs the candidates that the explanation of the "point within a circle" given by modern monitors (books of Masonic instruction) was not the original interpretation!

The lectures of Freemasonry give what modern monitors have made an exoteric explanation of the symbol, in telling us that the point represents the individual brother, the circle the boundary line of his duty to God and man, and the two perpendicular parallel lines the patron saints of the order—St. John the Baptist and St. John the Evangelist.
But that this was not always its symbolic signification we may collect from the true history of its connection with the phallus of the Ancient Mysteries. The phal-

lus was, among the Egyptians, the symbol of fecundity expressed by the male generative principle. It was communicated from the rites of Osiris to the religious festivals of Greece.[24]

A quick phone call to your local Lodge would reveal that the celebrated Masonic "Feasts of the Holy Saints John" are celebrated during the summer solstice and winter solstice periods. These important days fall respectively near or on June 21 and December 21.[25]

In a lecture on the 25th degree, or the Knight of the Brazen Serpent, Pike reveals the true meaning of the "point within a circle between two parallel lines" (which are permeated with astrology):

The Ancient Astronomers saw all the great Symbols of Masonry in the Stars. Sirius still glitters in our Lodge as the Blazing Star. The Sun is still symbolized by *the point within a circle*; and, with the Moon and Mercury or Anubis,[26] in the three Great Lights of the Lodge.[27] The Solstices, Cancer and Capricorn, the two Gates of Heaven, are the two pillars of Hercules, beyond which he, the Sun, never journeyed: and they still appear in our Lodges as the two great columns, Jachin and Boaz, and also as the *two parallel lines that bound the circle, with a point in the center,* emblem of the Sun, between the two tropics of Cancer and Capricorn[28] (italics mine).

Can you see in this example the "stratum theory" of Masonic symbolism? First, as an Entered Apprentice the Mason is told that he represents a point within the circle of conduct. Later he is told that the point within the circle represents the male reproductive organ, and finally he learns that the point actually represents the sun—as Osiris, Baal or Tammuz—in his journey between the tropics of Capricorn and Cancer.

Pretty bizarre, isn't it? I can't help but wonder where this leaves the Mason who believes that he is merely a point within a circle, when in fact he has been drawn into age-old lies perpetuated through ancient pagan fertility cults.

THE VOLUME OF SACRED LAW

The next three symbols, referred to as the "furniture of the Lodge" or the "Greater Lights" of Freemasonry, consist of the Volume of Sacred Law (VSL), and the Square and the Compass. Without them the Lodge cannot legally be held.[29]

As previously mentioned, a prerequisite to becoming a Mason is that you must believe in a god. Masonry, however, does not require that a man be a Christian to join. Many nineteenth-century Masonic writers emphatically state that Freemasonry is not a Christian organization. In fact, Christians I have met who have left Freemasonry inform me they were advised not to close their prayers "in Jesus' name" while praying in the Lodge to the Great Architect of the Universe (GAOTU). Because Freemasonry embraces men of all religions and thus many gods, a Mason may choose the Volume of Sacred Law (VSL) of the god he worships to be placed on the altar the night of his initiation. That VSL may be the Holy Bible, the Vedas, the Bhagavad Gita, the Koran or...

> The obligation of the candidate is always to be taken on the sacred book or books of his religion, that he may deem it more solemn and binding; and therefore it was that you were asked of what religion you were. We have no other concern with your religious creed.[30]

Recently, while talking with a Shriner on the East Coast, I raised this issue of Masonic deity and the VSL. His response was surprisingly clear and to the point. "You must believe in a god. Otherwise, when you took your oaths they wouldn't be binding." I wanted to shake the man and say, "Sir, listen to what you're saying!"

The Reverend J. T. Lawrence, author of many Masonic handbooks, informs us that according to a pronouncement of Grand Lodge, the Bible need not be in the Lodge at all.[31]

It is the custom of the Lodge in some nations to place on the altar the sacred books of all who are likely to attend that Lodge. "In a Lodge meeting on one occasion in Bombay there were among the [Brethren] present Christians, Hindus, Buddhists, Parsis, Jews, Sikhs, Muhammadans and Jains."[32] All these brothers knelt at a common altar and took binding oaths, cementing themselves into the order of the Mystic Tie.

Can't you just imagine the "spiritual free-for-all" that night, as each invoked the presence of deity?

THE SQUARE ON THE COMPASS

If preeminence were determined by visual placement, the sacred Scriptures would be the least of the three Great Lights, for the Square and Compass are placed upon the Volumes of Sacred Law. Never is the sacred Scriptures placed on top of the Square and Compass. For that matter, I have never seen a Masonic ring with an emblem of sacred Scriptures rather than the Square and Compass.

The Square and Compass are the two most commonly viewed mystical symbols of Freemasonry. In this first-degree tracing board, both tips of the compass are under the square. Mackey says it reminds the candidate that he is now dealing with the moral and political meaning of the symbols and not with their philosophical and spiritual meanings. The spiritual interpretations of these symbols are reserved for later. In the first degree, the Entered Apprentice receives this explanation:

> These two symbols combined teach us to square our actions and to keep them within due bounds.[33]

> As the Square represents our duties to our brothers, so the Compass gives that additional light which is to instruct us in the duty we owe ourselves.[34]

Azoth

From *Morals and Dogma of the Ancient and Accepted Scottish Rite of Freemasonry*
by Albert Pike, 1871, 1906.

Again, this explanation portrays the Square and Compass as symbols of harmless moral and philosophical concepts. After all, shouldn't we keep our actions within bounds? However, Pike begins to peel back the layers of deception as he explains their deeper meanings in a teaching of the 32nd degree. He suggests that the interpretation of these two symbols hearkens back to the sculpted images of the ancients. In describing a graphic printed in 1613 of an old Hermetic symbol entitled Azoth, Pike says:

> Upon it you see a triangle upon a square, both of these contained in a circle; and above this, standing upon a dragon, a human body, with two arms only, but two heads, one male and the other female. By the side of the male head is the Sun, and by that of the female head, the Moon, the crescent within the circle of the full moon. And the hand on the *male* side holds a *compass*, and that on the *female* side, a *square*....
>
> The hermaphroditic figure is the symbol of the double nature anciently assigned to the deity, as generator and producer, as Brahm and Maya among the Aryans, Osiris and Isis among the Egyptians. As the Sun was male, so the Moon was female; and Isis was both the sister and wife of Osiris. The Compass, therefore, is the Hermetic symbol of the creative deity, and the Square of the productive Earth or universe.[35]

Simply stated, as a 32° "Prince of the Royal Secret," the Mason is informed (that is, if he chooses to read the information available from the Lodge) of the true meaning of the Square and Compass present upon all sacred books on the altars of Freemasonry. They represent, in one sense, the male and female reproductive organs and, in another, the pagan solar deities Osiris and Isis!

The following are the words of a London financier, as told to Martin Short and recorded in his excellent book *Inside the Brotherhood*:

I became a Freemason in 1970, but even as I was going through the first degree ritual I had misgivings. It felt odd swearing that horrific oath on the Bible while a sharp compass point was thrust hard against my naked left breast. It felt odder still to be told to seal that oath by kissing the Bible, and then have my face thrust into the compass and square as they lay cradled in its open pages. It was only later that I realized that the compass and square were arranged in the shape of the vesica piscis [the womb] and the whole ceremony had sexual overtones.[36]

THE SUN, MOON AND STARS

The candidate is now ascending in his pursuit of "light" on the ladder of Masonic mystery. Who is the light at the top of this ladder? Could it possibly be none other than the sun god, by whatever name or silhouette, which was sought by the candidates of the ancient Mystery Religions? It is nothing less than bowing to the sun, moon and all the starry hosts—activities clearly forbidden in the Bible.

THE EAST, WEST, SOUTH AND NORTH

The four cardinal points—east, west, south and north—are closely associated with the above-mentioned symbol of the sun.

The east has always been considered peculiarly sacred. This was, without exception, the case in all the Ancient Mysteries. In the Egyptian rites, especially those of Adonis, which were among the earliest, and from which the others derived their existence, the Sun was the object of adoration, and his revolutions through the various seasons were fictitiously represented.[37]

These revolutions of the sun are represented today behind the closed doors of the Lodge. In a Masonic Lodge, the Worshipful Master always sits in the east, often with an image of the sun over his seat.

> The Master...in the east is a symbol of the rising sun; the Junior Warden in the south, of the meridian sun; and the Senior Warden in the west, of the setting sun.[38]

No one is ever seated in the north in a Masonic Lodge. It is the place where the sun seldom shines, and it represents the abode of darkness.

THE ALL-SEEING EYE

Plutarch said that the chief deity of Egypt was represented under the symbol of an eye. Masonic sources point out that such an emblem encompassed by solar flame recurs in the old theosophies.[39] The ancient Egyptian initiates saw the all-seeing eye as the emblem of Osiris, the creator![40] This symbol, often used in Freemasonry as the symbol of the omnipresent deity, is carried by literally millions of individuals every day. It is superimposed in the capstone of the pyramid on the back of our one-dollar bill. Although some contend that the all-seeing eye on the back of the dollar has no Masonic significance, others produce a convincing argument that the dollar bill contains numerous Masonic emblems, possibly dozens.

Masons also view the all-seeing eye of Masonry as the symbol of the creator god. Who is this creator god? A man who embraces Masonic philosophy may reply, "Who do you want it to be?"

Even with so brief a study of the main symbols of the first-degree tracing board, we can begin to see how a candidate might be confused or even deceived into seeking the light of Freemasonry.

Let us now continue with an even briefer look, a glance if you will, at the second- and third-degree tracing boards of the Craft.

THE SECOND—DEGREE TRACING BOARD

The second degree of Freemasonry, and thus the second-degree tracing board, is akin to the first. Both are preparatory to the third and final degree of Blue Lodge Masonry. (Blue Lodge Masonry consists only of the first three degrees.)

> The first degree in Masonry, like the lesser mysteries of the ancient systems of initiation, is only a preparation and purification for something higher. The Entered Apprentice is the child in Masonry. The lessons which he receives are simply intended to cleanse the heart and prepare the recipient for that mental illumination which is to be given in the succeeding degrees.[41]

The Entered Apprentice, now a candidate for the Fellowcraft degree, pauses at the foot of a winding staircase to ponder more of Masonry's arcane symbols. His search for light continues.

The activities of the Fellowcraft Mason are said to take place in the "middle chamber" of the temple. The principal symbols of this degree are displayed on the second-degree tracing board.

W. Kirk MacNulty, a Mason who writes on the symbolism of the tracing boards, suggests that the second-degree board is actually a detailed drawing of a part of the first—specifically, the point within a circle bounded by two parallel lines and Jacob's ladder.

> The two parallel lines are shown in the second degree as the two pillars...while the ladder is replaced on the second degree tracing board by the winding staircase. Like the ladder on the first degree board, the staircase extends in

the east-west direction and defines the 'dimension of consciousness' from materiality to divinity.[42]

Second Degree Tracing Board

From *Freemasonry: A Journey Through Ritual and Symbol* by W. Kirk MacNulty,
published by Thames and Hudson Inc., New York.
Copyright, and reproduced by permission, of the United Grand Lodge of England.

THE WINDING STAIRCASE

The staircase in this degree is always displayed as winding. It presents an aura of mystery because the candidate beginning his journey cannot foresee the rewards awaiting him in the middle chamber.

Masons teach that the first three degrees of Masonry correlate to an individual's journey from childhood through youth to manhood. If the Entered Apprentice is the child in Masonry, the Fellowcraft represents a young man starting on the journey of life, with the great task before him of self-improvement. On each step of the winding staircase, still traveling toward the east in search of light, the candidate pauses for instruction. He then continues his ascent of moral and spiritual development to a higher life.[43]

THE TWO COLUMNS AND GLOBES

Two columns, or pillars, topped with globes flank the winding staircase. To the casual observer these pillars may appear as twins; but if you look closely, you will see that the pillar on the left is topped with a terrestrial globe, while the pillar on the right supports a celestial globe containing the signs of the zodiac.

Albert Pike, along with other Masonic historians, equates these two pillars with the active and passive, or the male and female principles, as they relate to the heavenly (celestial) and earthly (terrestrial) realms. This is the monistic union of opposites idea in Hinduism, Buddhism and Taoism.

THE COMPASS AND SQUARE

In this tracing board there is another detail that may go unnoticed. One of the tips of the compass is now placed over the square. The candidate is becoming "enlightened." This Masonic enlightenment could be likened to a purification process where the aspirant shifts his focus from the physical earthly realm to matters of the spiritual domain. Thus he is more fully prepared for his induction into the mysteries of the Master Mason.

THE THIRD-DEGREE TRACING BOARD

THE COFFIN

The most obvious symbol in the Master Mason degree, as indicated on the third-degree tracing board, is the coffin. It is the analogue of the pastos, or coffin, in the Ancient Mysteries. This symbol represents a covenant with the grave.[44]

> The coffin in Masonry is found on tracing boards of the early part of the last century and has always constituted a part of the symbolism of the third degree, where the reference is precisely the same as that of the Pastos in the Ancient Mysteries.[45]

The coffin presented to Osiris by his brother Set was symbolic of the death and resurrection in the Egyptian Mysteries. Remember, the cults of the astral deities, i.e., the sun, moon and stars, were also fertility cults. The women in Ezekiel 8:14 wept over the death of Tammuz the sun god and thus bewailed the death and wilting of the vegetation in the winter, with its subsequent regeneration in the spring.

Through participation in the dramas of the Mystery Religions, the candidates reenacted the symbolic death, burial and resurrection of the fertility and astral deities, thus renewing a covenant with death and the grave. "The aspirant could not claim a participation until he had been placed in the pastos, or coffin. The act of placing him in the coffin was called the symbolic death in the Mysteries, and his deliverance was termed a *raising* from the dead"[46] (italics mine). Together with the sprig of acacia, the coffin symbolically teaches the great Masonic doctrine of a future life.[47]

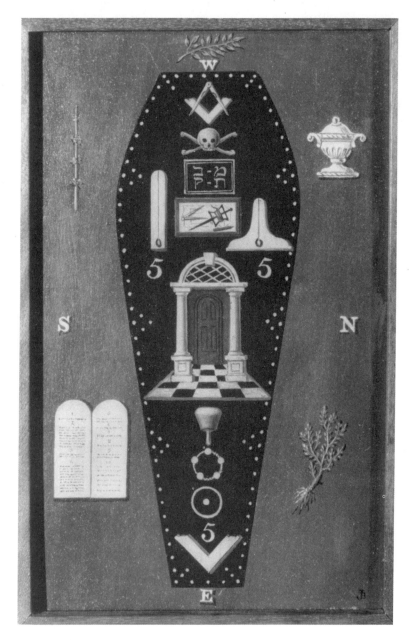

Third Degree Tracing Board

From *Freemasonry: A Journey Through Ritual and Symbol* by W. Kirk MacNulty,
published by Thames and Hudson Inc., New York.
Copyright, and reproduced by permission, of the United Grand Lodge of England.

THE ACACIA BRANCH

Above the coffin you will see the sprig of acacia. You will recall that in the legend of Osiris the sun god, the coffin was constructed of acacia. In the Hiramic legend, which we will discuss in the following chapter, a sprig of acacia was planted at the head of this Masonic hero-god. The acacia is part of the evergreen family. A sprig is placed into the third degree as a symbol of immortality. In its simplest significance, it represents to the Master Mason the hope of the immortality of the soul. It is intended to remind the Mason, by its evergreen nature, of that better and spiritual part within him that—as an emanation from the Great Architect of the Universe—can never die.[48]

Dr. Oliver, a nineteenth-century Masonic scholar, says that when a Master Mason exclaims, "My name is Acacia," it is equivalent to saying, "I have been in the grave—I have triumphed over it by rising from the dead. And being regenerated in the process, I have a claim to everlasting life."[49] If you have ever attended a funeral where Masons performed their mysterious rites, you may have noticed that they deposited a sprig of acacia in the grave of the deceased. However, there is another explanation of the symbol of the acacia.

In *Masonry Defined*, we learn that the acacia is also a symbol for initiation.

This is by far the most interesting of its interpretations, and was, we have every reason to believe, the primary and original, the others being incidental. It leads us at once to the investigation of the significant fact that in all the ancient initiations and religious mysteries there was some plant peculiar to each, which was consecrated by its own esoteric meaning, and which occupied an important position in the celebration of the rites, so that the plant, whatever it might be, from its constant and prominent use in the ceremonies of initiation, came at length to be adopted as the symbol of that initiation.[50]

I would like to draw your attention to an interesting and little-understood Scripture. In Ezekiel 8:17, after the Lord had taken Ezekiel past several abominable acts in the corrupted temple, including a group of men bowing toward the sun in the east, the Lord said to Ezekiel: "Look at them putting the branch to their nose!" The people in the temple were engaging in the idolatrous ceremonies and secret rituals of the Mystery Religions. In this context we may also infer that this strange act of putting the branch to the nose was part of those idolatrous rituals, and it displeased the Lord.

One could easily compare this "branch" of immortality of the Mystery Religions with the ankh of immortality that the goddess Isis held to the nose of her dead husband, Osiris.

THE COMPASS AND THE SQUARE

These two symbols maintain their same analogue as in the first two degrees, only now both tips of the Compass are placed on top of the Square. The candidate has progressed from the development of his lower, earthly nature to a higher, spiritual plane. He has traveled to the east in search of knowledge and has embraced the light of the Masonic Mysteries. The blindfold, which is part of all initiation rituals, is now removed from his eyes and he is worthy of the secrets of Freemasonry.

THE SKULL AND CROSSBONES

On the coffin is the skull and crossbones. Like the coffin, it is an emblem of mortality, alluding to the untimely death of Hiram Abif.[51]

THE PORCH, DORMER AND SQUARE PAVEMENT

These symbols are said to be the ornaments of a Master Mason's Lodge. "The porch was the entrance to the *sanctum sanctorum*, the dormer the window that gave light to the same, and the square pavement for the high priest to walk on."[52]

Every Mason who has taken the third degree should be familiar with the peculiar character and uses of the sanctum sanctorum, or holy of holies. "As it was the most sacred of the three parts of the temple, so has it been made symbolic of a Master's Lodge, in which are performed the most sacred rites of initiation in Ancient Craft Masonry."[53]

The holy of holies in the Gentile or pagan temple was referred to as the *Adytum*. The Adytum was also the most sacred and secret part of the Jewish temple. In both the Jewish and Gentile temples, the Adytum was accessible only to the priesthood. It was secluded and mysterious and never had windows.

Masonic authorities of the nineteenth century imply that the holy of holies of the Masonic Lodge more closely resembles the Adytum of the ancient pagan temples than that of the Jews or Gentiles.[54] In the Adytum of the pagan temple was a tomb or some relic or statue of the god to whom the temple was dedicated.

Freemasonry founded its third degree as the Adytum, or holy of holies, for all of its mysteries. "And therefore, in every Lodge of Master Masons there should be found, either actually or allegorically, a grave, or tomb, and coffin, because the third degree is the inmost sanctuary, the *kodesh kodashim*, the holy of holies of the Masonic temple."[55]

THE URN

There is a legend in some of the high degrees that suggests the heart of Hiram Abif was deposited in a golden urn and placed at the top of an obelisk.[56] Some lectures say that the ashes of Hiram were deposited in an urn.

THE CYPHER ON THE COFFIN

Walton Hannah, in his book *Darkness Visible,* states that "the cypher on the coffin is based on a simple noughts-and-crosses formula and reads as follows: on the plate, H.A.B. (for Hiram Abif), A(nno) L(ucis) 3000, flanked by T(ubal) C(ain). Beneath the skull is M. B. for the Third Degree word."[57] Anno Lucis means the "year of light"; the number 3000 refers to the Masonic hero-god Hiram Abif, slain 3,000 years after the creation of the world.

All of the symbols we have discussed in this chapter are inextricably linked to the rituals—the acted-out dramas—that we will explore in the next chapter. These rituals draw the initiate further into the depths of Freemasonry's arcane mysteries.

Notes

1. Albert Pike, *Morals and Dogma of the Ancient and Accepted Scottish Rite of Freemasonry* (Richmond, Va.: L. H. Jenkins, 1947), p. 22.
2. *Mystery:* The purpose of God, unknown to man except by revelation. This word was a popular, pagan religious term, used in the Mystery Religions to refer to secret information available to an exclusive group of people. Paul changes that meaning radically by always combining it with words such as "disclosed" (Col. 1:26), "made known" (Eph. 1:9), "make plain" (here), and "revelation" (Rom. 16:25). The Christian mystery is not secret knowledge for a few. It is revelation of divine truths "once hidden but *now openly proclaimed*" (italics mine). *NIV,* p. 1814.
3. Albert G. Mackey, *An Encyclopedia of Freemasonry,* Vol. 2 (New York and London: The Masonic History Company), p. 751.
4. Ibid., p. 752.
5. Ibid.
6. *What's a Mason?* (Silver Spring, Md.: Masonic Information Center, n.d.).

7. Mackey, *An Encyclopedia of Freemasonry*, p. 752.

8. W. Kirk MacNulty, *Freemasonry, A Journey Through Ritual and Symbol* (New York: Thames and Hudson, 1991), p. 7.

9. Pike, *Morals and Dogma*, pp. 104, 105, from a section of instruction to candidates of the Third Degree.

10. Mackey, *An Encyclopedia of Freemasonry*, Vol. 1, p. 17.

11. MacNulty, *Freemaonsry, A Journal*, p. 44.

12. Mackey, *An Encyclopedia of Freemasonry*, Vol. 2, p. 778.

13. Ibid., p. 501.

14. See 2 Corinthians 6:14.

15. Albert G. Mackey, *Masonry Defined* (Memphis, Tenn.: Masonic Supply Co., 1925), p. 100.

16. Robert Macoy, *A Dictionary of Freemasonry* (New York: Bell Publishing Company, 1989), p. 252.

17. Pike, *Morals and Dogma*, p. 14.

18. Mackey, *An Encyclopedia of Freemasonry*, Vol. 2, p. 798.

19. Ibid., *An Encyclopedia of Freemasonry*, Vol. 1, p. 149.

20. MacNulty, *Freemasonry, A Journal*, p. 20.

21. Mackey, *An Encyclopedia of Freemasonry*, Vol. 1, p. 81.

22. Malcolm C. Duncan, *Duncan's Ritual of Freemasonry* (New York: David McKay Company, n.d.), p. 53.

23. Mackey, *An Encyclopedia of Freemasonry*, Vol. 2, p. 202.

24. Ibid., p. 573.

25. The pagans had a fixed festival at each new moon: one at the summer and one at the winter solstice, as well as the vernal and autumnal equinoxes.

26. It has been said that Anubis is the son of Set and Nephthys, or possibly even Osiris and Nephthys. He is viewed in Egypt as the jackal god. It is in this sense that Pike seems to equate Anubis with the dog-star, Sirius.

27. Pike, *Morals and Dogma*, p. 486.

28. Ibid., p. 506.

29. C. W. Leadbeater, 33°, *The Hidden Life in Freemasonry* (Montana: Kessinger Publishing Company, n.d., formerly published by Theosophical Publishing House, 1928), p. 82.

30. Pike, *Morals and Dogma*, pp. 11, 12.

31. Leadbeater, *The Hidden Life in Freemasonry*, p. 82.

32. Ibid., (referring to comments by J. T. Lawrence, *Sidelights on Freemasonry*, p. 47).

33. Mackey, *An Encyclopedia of Freemasonry*, Vol. 2, p. 708.

34. Mackey, *An Encyclopedia of Freemasonry*, Vol. 1, p. 174.

35. Pike, *Morals and Dogma*, pp. 850, 851.

36. Martin Short, *Inside the Brotherhood* (New York: Dorset Press, 1989), p. 88.

37. Mackey, *An Encyclopedia of Freemasonry*, Vol. 1, p. 226.

38. Mackey, *Masonry Defined*, p. 234.

39. Arthur Edward Waite, *A New Encyclopaedia of Freemasonry* (New York: Wings Books), p. 21.

40. Mackey, *Masonry Defined*, p. 234.

41. Ibid., p. 211.

42. MacNulty, *Freemasonry, A Journal*, p. 23.

43. Mackey, *Masonry Defined*, p. 212.

44. The Mystery Religions exemplified the ancients' preoccupation with life after death. In their arcane ritual was found man's attempt to reach the divine; to provide answers to and protection from the uncertainties that lie beyond the grave. It is possible that this covenant with the grave is referred to by Isaiah the prophet in Isaiah 28:14,15.

45. Mackey, *Masonry Defined*, p. 349.

46. Ibid.

47. Ibid., p. 260.

48. Ibid., p. 51.

49. Ibid.

50. Ibid., p. 52.

51. Walton Hannah, *Darkness Visible* (London: Augustine Press, 1952), p. 147.

52. Ibid.

53. Mackey, *Masonry Defined*, p. 155.

54. Ibid.

55. Ibid., p. 156.

56. A trip to your local graveyard may reveal numerous obelisks, some topped with urns.

57. Hannah, *Darkness Visible*, p. 146.

CHAPTER SEVEN

Rites, Rituals and the "Raising" of a Master

Mr. [John Laurens], who has long been in darkness, now seeks to be brought to light and to receive a part in the rights and benefits of the Worshipful Lodge, erected to God and dedicated to the Saints John, as all brothers and fellows have done before.[1]

MALCOLM C. DUNCAN,
DUNCAN'S MASONIC RITUAL AND MONITOR

For you were once darkness, but now you are light in the Lord....Have nothing to do with the fruitless deeds of darkness, but rather expose them. For it is shameful even to mention what the disobedient do in secret.

APOSTLE PAUL, EPHESIANS 5:8,11,12

I have never been fond of rituals. They are usually repetitious and demand a great deal of memorization and attention to detail. In fact, after a few weeks of Cub Scouts I either resigned or flunked out, I don't remember which. I'm convinced that rituals get crossways with my visionary "big picture" kind of personality. If you're like me, you may find yourself easily bored and looking for a way of escape from certain types of ceremonial functions.

Having admitted that, I need you to accept an invitation to accompany me to an initiation in progress at our local Lodge. If it appears to you to be a little dry, that's OK; most Masons who have passed through this initiation ritual would be quick to agree with you. However, I must caution you to avoid the temptation to equate "boring" with "insignificant."

The legends of Freemasonry, like the one we're about to view, are also referred to in the symbolism of Freemasonry. "The legends of Masonry are parables, and a parable is only a spoken symbol."[2] These legends, or "spoken symbols," are acted out behind the closed doors of the Lodge in the form of strange rites and ritual dramas. In the lower degrees, Masons are cast as the legendary Masonic hero-gods. In the higher degrees, the candidates usually view these ancient ritualistic dramas, though they may be cast as characters in the plays as well.

Now let me introduce you to Pastor John Laurens, who will soon be initiated into the third degree of Masonry. He is a young preacher who recently graduated from seminary and is enjoying his first pastorate at a little church in the southeastern United States. One Sunday, following a morning service, a deacon meets Pastor John at the door and invites him to meet a few of his buddies. They are all introduced as belonging to an organization that "makes good men better." Based on his acquaintance with these men, Pastor John decides to join the local Lodge.

Since joining, he has "entered" the First Degree of Freemasonry as an Apprentice and has subsequently "passed" a

Fellowcraft in the Second Degree. Tonight we will see him initiated into the Third Degree and "raised" a Master Mason.

In reality we would not be allowed to observe this ritual. It is one of the esoteric ceremonies of the Craft and, therefore, attended only by the initiates of Freemasonry. I will reconstruct the scenes from information gathered from ritual monitors and interviews with former Masons. The ritual we will witness is a very important Masonic tradition through which all Masons must pass.

THE THIRD DEGREE

The Third Degree is said to be the most sublime of all the degrees in Freemasonry, and being "raised" to the degree of Master Mason is one of the most significant initiations through which Pastor John will pass. It is pending the ritual of this degree that the blindfold is finally removed and Pastor John will become "enlightened." As a Master Mason, he will then be worthy of the deep secrets of Freemasonry.

THE PREPARATION

Before we actually see Pastor John Laurens enter the Lodge, he is duly prepared in an anteroom. He is divested of all his clothing and given a pair of drawers, or pajama-like clothes, to put on. Both legs of his drawers are turned above the knees, thus exposing his knees, legs and feet. He is also divested of anything metallic, including his wedding ring.

A hoodwink, or blindfold, is placed over Pastor John's eyes. After being securely tethered to a cable tow—a rope tied three times around his body—he is again led, as in the first two degrees from the preparation room to the door of the Lodge. His guide knocks three times, and from inside the Lodge comes the response: "What do you seek?"

In the first degree his guide replies for him:

> [Brother Laurens], who has long been in darkness, and now seeks to be brought to light and to receive a part in the rights and benefits of the Worshipful Lodge, erected to God and dedicated to the Saints John, as all brothers and fellows have done before.[3]

Now, in the third degree, Pastor John's response is simply, "More light!" The Lodge door is opened and we finally see him as he is escorted into the Lodge.

THE RITE OF INDUCTION

Within six to eight feet inside the Lodge door, our pastor friend is stopped. An open Compass is pressed to his naked breast. He is told by the Senior Deacon: "[Brother Laurens], upon your first admission into a Lodge of Master Masons, I receive you on the points of the Compass extending from your naked right to left breast which is to teach you that as most vital parts of man are contained within the breasts, so are the most excellent tenets of our institution contained within the points of the Compass, which are *friendship, morality and brotherly love*."[4]

THE RITE OF CIRCUMAMBULATION

We now see Pastor Laurens being conducted, still blindfolded and tied, three times around the Lodge room, traveling in a clockwise direction. As they pass the different stations, the Senior Warden in the west, the Worshipful Master in the east and the Junior Warden in the south all give a single rap. On the second trip, each gives two raps, and on the third, three raps each. As Pastor John is being led on his symbolic pilgrimage, we can hear the Master or Chaplain reading from the first to the seventh verses of the twelfth chapter of Ecclesiastes.

Pastor John finally ends up at the altar where he is met by the Worshipful Master. "[Brother Laurens]," the Master says, "you are now at the altar of Masonry for the third time; but before proceeding further, it becomes my duty, as the Worshipful Master of this Lodge, to inform you that it will be necessary that you take upon yourself a solemn oath or obligation pertaining to this degree. *And I can assure you, upon the honor of a man and Mason, that in this obligation there is nothing that will conflict with any duty you owe to God, your country, your family, your neighbor or yourself.*"5

We then observe Pastor John as he kneels on his bare knees, with his hands resting on the Holy Bible, Compass and Square.

THE RITE OF SECRECY

The Master now gives three raps, and all the other Brethren move to the altar and form two lines extending from west to east. The Master also approaches the altar and we hear him as he directs Pastor John in the Master Mason's obligation. This obligation is quite lengthy and includes matters of secrecy, Lodge support and assistance to fellow Masons. It cautions Pastor John regarding his involvement in clandestine Lodges where women and atheists are present. It also admonishes him in matters of cheating, fidelity and falsely using the Masonic Grand Hailing sign of a Master Mason or the sign of distress. Furthermore, Pastor John is warned to not give the Grand Masonic word in any other manner or form than he has received it. Finally, he must bind himself by repeating the following oath:

All this, I [John Laurens] most solemnly, sincerely promise and swear, with a firm and steady resolution, to perform the same, without any hesitation, mental reservation, or secret evasion of mind whatever, binding myself,
under no less penalty than that of having my body severed
in two, my bowels taken from thence and burned to ashes,
the ashes scattered before the four winds of heaven, that
no more remembrance might be had of so vile and wicked
a wretch as I would be, would I ever, knowingly, violate
this my Master Mason's obligation. So help me God, and
keep me steadfast in the due performance of the same.[6]

We see Pastor John now kiss the Volume of Sacred Law upon
which are deposited the Compass and Square. We hear the
Worshipful Master say to the Senior Deacon: "Brother Senior
Deacon, you will release the brother from the cable tow. *He is
bound to us by obligation, a tie stronger than human hands can impose*"[7]
(italics mine). The cable tow around John's waist is now removed.

THE RITE OF ILLUMINATION
"[Brother Laurens]," the Worshipful Master asks, "in your present condition, what do you most desire?"

"Further light in Masonry," we hear Pastor John reply.

As the Worshipful Master quickly removes the hoodwink, we
hear him say, "Let there be light!"

THE RITE OF ENTRUSTING
Pastor John is now entrusted with the pass grip of a Master
Mason. Between a flow of unusual syllables echoed between the
Worshipful Master and the Senior Deacon, he learns that this
grip has a name, "Tubal-Cain."[8]

After we hear the Master deliver his concluding remarks
about Tubal-Cain, he gives one rap of his gavel and the Lodge is

seated. Pastor John is then escorted to the Senior Deacon where he is taught to wear his apron as a Master Mason.

THE RITE OF INVESTITURE

"My brother," says the Senior Warden, "Masonic tradition informs us that at the building of Solomon's Temple, Master Masons wore their aprons with the corner turned down in the form of a square to designate them as Master Masons or overseers of the work. As a speculative Master Mason you will therefore wear yours in like manner."

Besides learning the new way to wear his apron, Pastor John is now entitled to the working tool of a Master. "The working tools of a Master Mason are all of the implements of Masonry indiscriminately, but more especially the trowel." While operative Masons used the trowel to spread the cement that unites the building into one common mass, "we use it for a more noble purpose of spreading the cement of brotherly love and affection—that cement which unites us into one sacred band or society of friends."[9]

Pastor John is now taken to the anteroom from whence he came, and he is reinvested of all that he had been previously divested.

The "Raising" of John Laurens

From this point forward, the ritual through which our pastor friend passes becomes even more peculiar. While the initiate is in the anteroom, the Lodge is made ready for the remaining portion of the ceremony of initiation.

> A canvas, seven feet long and about six feet wide, with five or six long loops on each side, is produced from a closet or chest in the room; and a buckskin bag stuffed with hair, about the size of two boxing gloves, is taken from the same receptacle....The room is cleared by removing the altar and lights and the two large pillars used in the second degree.[10]

The door of the Lodge is unceremoniously thrown open, and we again see our friend Pastor John Laurens, wearing his new Senior Warden's jewel. He is permitted to enter. After congratulations, his friends approach him as if to signify that there is no more ceremony. We hear the Worshipful Master give one rap of his gavel and it appears they are ready to close the Lodge. Before they do, however, our friend is asked to approach the east. He is escorted by the conductor, who then positions himself behind the candidate with a hoodwink secreted in his pocket.

The Worshipful Master then informs Pastor John that he is not yet a Master Mason and may never become one. He must prove how well he will withstand the amazing trials that will soon be disclosed to him.

> You have a rough and rugged road to travel, beset with thieves, robbers and murderers; and should you lose your life in the attempt, it will not be the first instance of the kind, my brother....Heretofore, you have had someone pray for you, but now you have none. You must pray for yourself. You will therefore suffer yourself to be again hoodwinked, and kneel where you are, and pray orally or mentally, as you please. When through, signify by saying Amen, and arise and pursue your journey.[11]

The room is darkened and the conductor takes Pastor John by the right arm. They circle the room three times in a clockwise direction. As they walk, we hear the conductor relate to John the strange Masonic myth of Hiram Abif. As they approach the stations in the south and west, the Junior Warden and Senior Warden impersonate two ruffians and rough him up. Finally, our hoodwinked pastor friend is rushed to the east where the Worshipful Master, acting as another ruffian with a setting maul, strikes a blow to his head. We now discover our friend Pastor John Laurens lying on the floor of the Lodge, symbolically dead.

The rest of this peculiar ceremony is the unfolding drama of the legend of Hiram Abif, with Pastor John Laurens cast as the legendary, mystical Masonic hero-god, Hiram. We see him symbolically murdered, buried and raised. He is killed by the Worshipful Master, dragged to the northeast corner of the Lodge where he is buried in the "rubbish of the temple," and then dragged back to the feet of the Worshipful Master.

Now picture this: The Worshipful Master, who just symbolically murdered our pastor friend, now stands at his feet and asks, "In whom do you trust?" Pastor John replies, "In God we trust," whereby the Worshipful Master reaches down his hand and "raises" him with the strong grip of the lion's paw, the grip of a Master Mason. The blindfold is removed and our friend is now worthy of the deep secrets of Freemasonry.

From Darkness to Light?

To the casual observer, this ritual may appear completely harmless—certainly weird, maybe a little confusing, definitely boring, but basically harmless. However, before you draw hasty conclusions, I challenge you to ponder a few actions and statements made by our dear friend Pastor John Laurens.

First, consider the question our pastor was asked before he could enter the Masonic Lodge: "What do you seek?" Then consider carefully our pastor's memorized response: "I am in the darkness and I need the light of Freemasonry!" Doesn't this response from a pastor, or any Christian believer for that matter, strike you as rather odd?

Scriptures inform us that Jesus is the "light of the world."[12] If I have the light of Christ in my heart, yet I am seeking light, doesn't this suggest there must be another light? Or at least more light?

Pastor John was then escorted around the room clockwise—in the direction the sun rises and sets. He paused at the stations in the east, west and south in this symbolic journey in search of light. As we learned from the tracing boards in the preceding chapters, the Lodge officers in these three stations represent the sun in its rising, high meridian and setting.

When Pastor John finally bowed at the Masonic altar, it was intentional that he was bowing to the east, to the station of the Worshipful Master, symbol of the sun (see Ezek. 8:16).

On this altar was his choice of the Volume of Sacred Law, but on this holy book were placed the Masonic symbols of the Square and Compass. The candidate gets to choose his sacred book, but he cannot choose to remove or retain these two symbols. In the previous chapter we learned that many Masonic scholars more than suggest that these two emblems represent the ancient solar deities of Osiris and Isis. They also represent the male and female reproductive organs. To this arrangement our pastor bowed to the east and swore his allegiance to the GAOTU, the god of Freemasonry. Do you sense something seriously wrong with this picture?

Second, note that immediately after Pastor John's response, "In God we trust," he was "raised" into the mysteries of Masonry. He participated in a symbolic resurrection and his blindfold was removed. Into what, or more accurately, into whom was our friend raised, or resurrected?

The Master Mason participates in a dramatic reenactment of the Masonic hero-god, Hiram Abif, as clearly seen in the "raising" of Pastor John Laurens. Let's take a look at this legend.

The Legend of Hiram Abif

I was introduced to the legend of this Masonic hero-god in 1993 while visiting a Scottish Rite Temple in south Texas. I was drawn to a painting in the foyer depicting the dedication of Solomon's Temple. In this painting was Solomon surrounded by his stonemasons, and next to Solomon was a figure named Hiram Abif. The caption informed me that it was Hiram reminding Solomon that if it were not for his Masons, the temple would yet be incomplete. Solomon responded in the affirmative and deferred the seat of privilege to Hiram.

There is no character in the annals of Freemasonry more significant than Hiram Abif. According to Masonic lore, Hiram Abif was the mythical Grand Master at the building of Solomon's Temple. Here is the basic story.

THE DEATH

In the legend, 15 Fellowcrafts, who see the temple about to be completed, conspire to extort from their Grand Master, Hiram Abif, the secrets of a Master Mason and then to take his life. It was Hiram's custom to enter the sanctum sanctorum, or holy of holies, at high 12, to offer up his devotion to the deity and draw his designs on the trestle board.

Of the 15 ruffians, 12 recant and 3 persist in their murderous design. These 3 place themselves at the south, west and east gates of the inner court of the temple and await Hiram's return. The first ruffian thrice demands of him the secrets of the Master Mason. Upon his refusal, the ruffian gives him a blow across his throat with the 24-inch gauge. Hiram staggers to the west where he is likewise accosted by the second. His refusal this time brings a blow from a Square across his breast, whereupon he flees to the east gate. He is met there by a violent blow from a setting maul and falls dead on the spot.

THE BURIAL

The ruffians bury the body in the rubbish of the temple until at low 12 (12 at night), they convey it westerly to the brow of a hill west of Mount Moriah. There they dig a grave due east and west, and at the head plant an acacia tree to conceal it.

The next day Hiram is found to be missing. King Solomon, being informed and fearful of some fatal accident, orders a roll call of the workmen. Three Fellowcrafts are also missing, namely, Jubelo, Jubela and Jubelum. King Solomon orders the 12 remaining Fellowcrafts who had recanted to go in search of the body. They begin the search; and while returning after several days of fruitless search, one brother, more weary than the others, sits down on a hill west of Mount Moriah to rest. On attempting to rise, he catches hold of the sprig of acacia, which easily gives way and arouses his curiosity. Upon examination, the Fellowcrafts find the appearance of a new grave.

THE OATHS

While meditating on this singular circumstance, the Fellowcrafts hear the following horrid prayers coming from the cleft of an adjacent rock. The first is the voice of Jubelo:

> Oh that my throat had been cut across, my tongue torn out by the roots and buried in the rough sands of the sea at low water mark, where the tide ebbs and flows twice in twenty-four hours, ere I had been the accessory to the death of so great a man as our Grand Master Hiram Abif![13]

The second is the voice of Jubela, who exclaims:

> Oh that my left breast had been torn open, my heart plucked out and given as prey to the beasts of the fields

and the fowls of the air, ere I had consented to the death of so good a man as our Grand Master Hiram Abif![14]

Finally, the third voice, that of Jubelum, cries out in tones of greater horror than the others:

Oh that my body had been severed in twain, my bowels taken from thence and burned to ashes and the ashes scattered to the four winds of heaven, so that no trace or remembrance might be had of so vile and perjured a wretch as I. It was I who gave the fatal blow that caused the death of our Grand Master Hiram Abif.[15]

Upon hearing these confessions, the Fellowcrafts rush in, seize and bind the three ruffians and take them to King Solomon, who after their confessions orders them executed after the manner of their several imprecations.

The 12 Fellowcrafts are then ordered to search near the body and to observe if anything of the Master's word or anything appertaining to the Master's degree is on or about it. The body is discovered in a westerly course from the temple in a grave dug due east and west. Nothing is found but the jewel of his office, which designates the body.

THE RAISING

King Solomon orders the twelve Fellowcrafts to go and assist in raising the body. Because the Master's word was lost, it is agreed between Solomon and Hiram, King of Tyre, that the first sign given on arriving at the grave and the first word spoken after the body is raised should be adopted as the sign and word for the regulation of all Master's Lodges until future generations should find out the right word.

At the grave, King Solomon orders one of the Fellowcrafts to take the body by the Entered Apprentice grip and see if it can be raised; but owing to the high state of putrefaction, the body having already been dead fifteen days, the skin slips and the body cannot be raised.

King Solomon then requests that Hiram, King of Tyre, take the body by the Fellowcraft grip and see if it can be raised. But owing to the reasons already assigned, the body cannot be raised.

When King Solomon takes the body by the strong grip of a Master Mason, or the "Lion's Paw," and raises it on the five points of fellowship, the Fellowcrafts then convey it back to the temple area and bury it.

Who Is Hiram?

The *historical* Hiram was a craftsman highly skilled in working with brass.[16] Scripture says that he was also "trained to work in gold and silver, bronze and iron, stone and wood, and with purple and blue and crimson yarn and fine linen...experienced in all kinds of engraving and [could] execute any design given to him" (2 Chron. 2:14).

The *legendary* Hiram is represented as being a great architect, superintending the building and drawing out the plans of the temple. According to Scripture, the real Hiram finished all his labors in and around the temple,[17] while the mystical Hiram of Masonic tradition is represented as "having lost his life in a singular manner just before the completion of the temple, and with some of his designs unfinished."[18]

Well then, who is this mystical Hiram? You might be surprised at his true identity as revealed not just by this author but by Masonic scholars as well. The following is a quote from *The Illustrated History of Freemasonry*, with punctuation and capitalized words copied exactly as written.

The twelve Fellowcrafts who were deputed for this service (search for Grand Master Hiram) represented the twelve signs of the zodiac; one of whom would be sure to find their Grand Master Hiram—*the personification of Osiris, the Sun.*

It may be remarked that the lamentations uttered for the death of the Grand Master Hiram is in exact accordance with the customs of the Egyptians, in their celebrations of the fabled death of Osiris, the Sun; of the Phoenicians, for the loss of Adonis, and of the Greeks, in their mystic rites of the Eleusinian Ceres.

The strong paw of the lion wrests Osiris from the clutches of Typhon and places him in his wonted course, the archetype of the rising of Grand Master Hiram by the Strong Grip of Lion's Paw[19] (italics mine).

A very limited knowledge of the history of the primitive worships and mysteries is necessary to enable any person to recognize in the Master Mason Hiram, *the Osiris of the Egyptians,* the Mithras of the Persians, the Bacchus of the Greeks, and the Atys of the Phrygians, of which these people celebrated the passion, death and resurrection....*In an astronomical connection, Hiram is representative of the Sun,* the symbol of his apparent progress, which appearing at the south gate, so to speak, is smote downward and more downward as he advances toward the west, which passing, he is immediately vanquished and put to death by darkness represented, in following the same allegory, by the spirits of evil; but returning, he rises again, conqueror and resurrected[20] (italics mine).

Here is another way we can view this significant ritual of the third degree through which all Masons must pass. Architects design and build things. The GAOTU (Great Architect of the Universe) of Freemasonry also designs and builds things. He builds temples. Carved into a frieze over the threshold of the House of the Temple in Washington, D.C., you will find these enlightening words:

> Freemasonry builds its temples in the hearts of men and among nations.

Is it possible that the newly "raised" Master Mason, now shaped into the smooth ashlar, is cemented into the temple that the GAOTU is designing and building? I believe so, and this is a very serious matter. What if the god of the Lodge is not the God of Abraham, Isaac and Jacob? What if he is not the Father of our Lord and Savior, Jesus Christ?

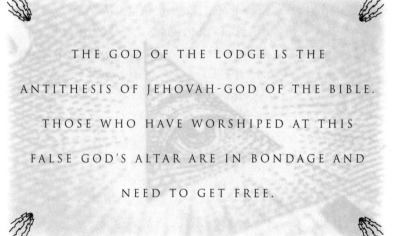

THE GOD OF THE LODGE IS THE ANTITHESIS OF JEHOVAH-GOD OF THE BIBLE. THOSE WHO HAVE WORSHIPED AT THIS FALSE GOD'S ALTAR ARE IN BONDAGE AND NEED TO GET FREE.

I believe that the god of the Lodge is the antithesis of Jehovah-God of the Bible, and those who have worshiped at this false god's altar are in bondage and need to get free.

Let's now move on to the next section of this book and learn how we can chisel our loved ones free from this mystical temple that the god of Freemasonry is designing and building.

Notes

1. Malcolm C. Duncan, *Duncan's Ritual of Freemasonry* (New York: David McKay Company, n.d.), p. 29
2. Albert G. Mackey, *An Encyclopedia of Freemasonry*, Vol. 2 (New York: The Masonic History Company, 1915), p. 752.
3. Duncan, *Duncan's Ritual of Freemasonry*, p. 29
4. Edmond Ronayne, *Handbook of Freemasonry* (Chicago, Ill.: Ezra A. Cook Publications, 1962), p. 164.
5. Ibid., p. 169
6. Duncan, *Duncan's Ritual of Freemasonry*, p. 96.
7. Ronayne, *Handbook of Freemasonry*, p. 173.
8. "That Tubal-Cain gave first occasion to the name and worship of Vulcan hath been probably conceived both from the very great affinity of the names, and that Tubal-Cain expressly mentioned to be an instructor of every artificer in brass and iron; and as near relation as Apollo had to Vulcan, Jubal had to Tubal-Cain, who was the inventor of music, or the father of all such as handle the harp and organ, which the Greeks attribute to Apollo." Mackey, *An Encyclopedia of Freemasonry*, Vol. 2, pp. 807, 808.
9. Ronayne, *Handbook of Freemasonry*, p. 179.
10. Duncan, *Duncan's Ritual of Freemasonry*, p. 100.
11. Ibid., p. 102.
12. John 8:12; 9:5; 12:46; 1 John 1:5.
13. Similar to Entered Apprentice oath.
14. Similar to Fellowcraft oath.
15. Similar to Master Mason oath.
16. Hiram is described as being filled with wisdom, and understanding, and cunning to work all works in brass (see 1 Kings 7:13). According to 2 Chronicles 2:13,14, Hiram was also skilled in gold, silver, iron, stone and timber, and in various colors of linen and all manner of decoration.
17. See 2 Chronicles 4:11.
18. Moses W. Redding, *The Illustrated History of Freemasonry* (New York: Redding & Co., 1901), p. 170.

19. Ibid., p. 88.

20. Emmanuel Rebold, *A General History of Freemasonry* (Cincinnati: American Masonic Publishing Association, 1868), p. 392.

CHAPTER EIGHT

THE TRUTH WILL MAKE YOU FREE

Masonry...uses false explanations and misinterpretations of its symbols to mislead those who deserve only to be misled; to conceal the Truth, which it calls Light, from them, and to draw them away from it. Truth is not for those who are unworthy or unable to receive it, or would pervert it.[1]

ALBERT PIKE,
MORALS AND DOGMA OF THE ANCIENT AND ACCEPTED SCOTTISH RITE OF FREEMASONRY

If you hold to my teaching, you are really my disciples. Then you will know the truth, and the truth will set you free.

JESUS, JOHN 8:31,32

In chapters 1 through 7 of this book, I introduced the pagan roots of Freemasonry and the secret oaths and rituals acted out behind the closed doors of the Lodge. It was heavy stuff, and if you feel overwhelmed, cheer up. It's now time to move on to the "So what can we do about it?" section.

In chapters 9 and 10 we will learn how the generational curses of Freemasonry affect the families of Lodge members and how we can break free from their deadly grip. Before we do that

I would like to direct this chapter to those who are still entangled in the insidious web of Freemasonry. How does a person get free?

I can't think of a better way to introduce this chapter than to share the story of a man who got free from Freemasonry. The following is an excerpt from a letter I received in the fall of 1998 from a man named Mike. Testimonies like his encourage me, and I trust this letter will bring you hope as well.

Dear Friends,

Many of you were surprised to hear that after 21 years of involvement, including serving as Worshipful Master, I have demitted from all Masonic bodies. Those of you who knew me from the Lodge knew also that I was zealous for the order and served with enthusiasm for most of those years.

I believed there was only one God who was known by many different names and that it didn't matter what religion you belonged to, they all led to the same God. Weren't they all teaching morality? Wasn't this the goal of religion? I had no idea what idolatry was, or for that matter, any of those other church words. I realized that I had never taken the time to consider who God was, my relationship to Him, or the implications of my Masonic involvement.

My pastor handed me some research done by Ron Campbell, then continued to track my progress. He knew how to confront with love. I proceeded to verify Ron's teachings by looking up his sources and reading them for myself. This study took me over three years. I recalled my Masonic experiences, studied mythology, looked up lots of words in the dictionary and read from books such as *Morals and Dogma* by Albert Pike, a noted Masonic scholar.

One day it all became crystal clear. It was like someone had removed a blindfold from my eyes. Why hadn't I been able to see this before? It was so plain, so simple. What I saw in Pike's book finally hit home. I got a sickening feeling in the pit of my stomach. It was all true. I had been deceived and had tried so hard to justify myself. I was wrong. I finally understood that this was idolatry and that idolatry is unfaithfulness to God, just the same as adultery is unfaithfulness to your spouse.

With the truth now revealed, I had no other recourse but to renounce Freemasonry and withdraw my membership from all of its bodies.[2]

I'm sure you're wondering, as many of Mike's friends and loved ones did, what took him so long to see the truth. I have some thoughts on this that I will share in the next chapter, but the most important fact to remember for now is that Mike *did* find the truth. He discovered that Freemasonry was idolatry. Rather than leading him to the true light, it deceptively drew him further from it. Knowing this truth led Mike to heartfelt repentance and renunciation, which ultimately led to his complete freedom.

Why Does Anyone Need Freedom from Freemasonry?

A number of years ago, Darla and I participated in a prayer group in Texas. During one meeting it was voiced that Brian, a member of the group, had been a Mason.

"Oh," Darla said, "then you've renounced your involvement in the Lodge?"

Brian's rebuttal was quick and harsh. "Renounced? I have nothing to renounce! Freemasonry brought me closer to my God!"

Brian's response revealed that he had either not truly left the Lodge or that he had left it for the wrong reason. (It's sometimes easier to get the Mason out of the Lodge than it is to get the Lodge out of the Mason.)

Most Masons, whether active or nonactive, would pose a question similar to Brian's: Why in the world would I want to be free from Freemasonry? Masonry takes good men and makes them better!

You see, it's possible to be in bondage and not even realize it. It is only when this blindfold is removed, as Mike so clearly stated in his letter, that a man can see Masonry for what it is—idolatry. And when it is clearly seen as such, the most effective tool we have to break its stronghold on our families and us is heartfelt repentance.

Incidentally, when addressing the issue of Masonic involvement, it is important to understand that a man either is or is not a Mason. There is no middle ground. Either he is in or he is out, and thus he is either in bondage to the god of the Lodge or he is free. Please understand that even a nonactive Mason (like Brian) is still a Mason and needs to be set free. Unless a Mason has repented, renounced and resigned from the Lodge, he is still in danger of all the pain that idolatry has to offer. I'll share more about this in the final chapter.

WHAT YOU DON'T KNOW CAN HURT YOU!

I can't believe I used to say, "What you don't know can't hurt you." I'm now convinced that if "what we don't know" is the truth, our ignorance could be costly. In other words, sometimes the truth hurts; however, not knowing the truth hurts even worse, because our adversary takes advantage of our ignorance. Second Corinthians 2:11 (*NASB*) records the words: "In order that no advantage be taken of us by Satan; for we are not ignorant of his schemes." From this we may infer that if it is not God's desire for us to be ignorant of Satan's schemes, then He is willing to reveal those schemes to us.

Ignorance of truth keeps us in bondage, but knowing the truth sets us free. Jesus said in John 8:32: "You will know the truth, and the truth will set you free." Put another way, *the truth you know* will set you free.

Did you know that truth is not altered by our ignorance of it or changed one iota by our denial or rejection of it? Nor does the truth change when it is cloaked by a veil of deception. Truth needs no defense, and the opinions of man cannot alter it.

During the 21 years of Mike's involvement in the Lodge, the truth of Freemasonry remained steadfast; Mike's ignorance, opinions or rejection of it did not alter it. Rather, it was when Mike aligned himself with the plumb line of truth that *he* changed.

We can view the truth from two perspectives. First, we can know the truth *about* a particular subject or person; and second, we can actually *know* the subject, who is a person. Let me explain.

First, when we know about the truth about a subject—in this case Freemasonry—our freedom begins. After speaking in churches and conferences, I've been approached by those who said they felt strongholds begin to break in their lives simply as a result of knowing the truth about Freemasonry. The truth they now know is setting them free. While it's important to be knowledgeable about the truth of Freemasonry, it doesn't guarantee a man's freedom. A man can receive head knowledge about the truth and never be changed. This brings us to our second perspective.

To know the truth includes more than knowing *about* the truth. There is a more intimate aspect of "to know," as in actually knowing the Truth (with a capital *T*). That is, rather than just knowing about a subject, you know the subject, or the person, who is Truth.

Jesus said, "I am the way, and the truth, and the life" (John 14:6, *NASB*). In this case, knowing the Truth infers "experiential" intimacy. It is more than knowing *about* Jesus. To know the Truth, one must experience the Truth; one must believe Him, embrace Him and be obedient to Him. You see, knowing the Truth not only involves head knowledge but a heart posture as well! It is this kind of *knowing the truth* that will set men free, particularly as it relates to the stronghold of Freemasonry.

What Is the Truth of Freemasonry?

By now you should understand what thousands before me have discovered—Freemasonry is nothing less than blatant idolatry. This book was not intended to be simply an exposé of Freemasonry, but rather a book on how to get free from Freemasonry. However, it was necessary to first expose the truth that Masonic historians and Christian ministers have voiced for centuries. After all, why would a man choose to free himself from something he doesn't know he's in bondage to?

When the veil of deception is ripped from Freemasonry, the secret exposed is not merely the Masonic grips and phrases. The secret is not even one of intrigue as men act out the thrilling drama of a cloak-and-dagger spy novel. The truth revealed is one of pain and disappointment to find that through Freemasonry, men we care for have been ensnared by the same seducing spirits that operated behind the myth and idolatry of the ancient Mideast.

İDOLATRY İS A DOUBLE-EDGED SWORD

For anyone to engage in any form of idolatry is spiritually dangerous, if not deadly, because it involves broken covenants and fractured relationships at the highest level. It is blatant disobedience to the first two of the Ten Commandments found in Exodus 20: "You shall have no other gods before me," and "You shall not make for yourself an idol." You see, when we disobey, it's not as though we remain on neutral ground. We don't just miss the blessings. When we are guilty of idolatry, we not only don't get the good, but we must take the bad as well. We've lost the blessings and gained the judgments and curses.

In this sense, idolatry is a double-edged sword. The first edge severs from man all the covenantal blessings of God listed in Deuteronomy 28:1-14. Simply stated, when a man is disobedient and embraces idolatry, he obstructs the blessings of God in his life. Idolatry alters God's destiny and purposes for him. I would go so far as to suggest that Freemasonry actually hinders revival in his life.

The second edge of idolatry's double-edged sword clears the way for judgment. Scripture clearly reveals that consequential judgment always follows in the wake of idolatry (see Deut. 28:15-68). These judgments often manifest themselves in the form of curses on our families and our nations. And more often than not these curses are not merely the fruit of what we sow, but they also include spiritual bondages that can only be released by claiming the power of the blood of Christ.

The choice is completely ours. We can choose either blessings or curses, life or death.[3] I've learned that indeed it is God's heart to bless a man and his family. However, He is sometimes limited by *our* poor choices.

HEART-TO-HEART

With the help of the Holy Spirit, I would like to share heart-to-heart with you men who are still in the Lodge. I want to share with you God's heart on the matter of idolatry and thus what I believe to be His heart on Freemasonry. On occasion I will use the words "idolatry" and "Freemasonry" interchangeably.

I've made it clear in the previous chapters that God hates idolatry. Does this mean He hates us when we engage in idolatrous practices? Quite the contrary. He hates idolatry because He loves us so deeply, and idolatry separates us from Him.

IDOLATRY IS NOT JUST GIVING YOURSELF
OVER TO OTHER GODS BUT ALSO ALLOWING
YOUR HEART TO BE CAPTURED BY ANYONE
OR ANYTHING OTHER THAN GOD. IT IS
SPIRITUAL ADULTERY.

Idolatry is a heart issue. It involves relationship, love and intimacy. It is not just giving yourself over to other gods but also allowing your heart to be captured by anyone or anything other than God. It is spiritual adultery.

Do you remember Mike's confession in our introductory story? He said, "I was wrong. I finally understood that [Masonry] was idolatry and that idolatry is unfaithfulness to God, just the same as adultery is unfaithfulness to your spouse." Like an adulterous affair, Freemasonry breaks the heart of our heavenly Father.

COMPLACENCY BY COEXISTENCE

Many Masons I have met seem to be complacent about spiritual matters; that is, their spiritual discernment has been somewhat dulled. I can't help wondering if the complacency in the Church in America is partially due to the fact that we are coexisting with Freemasonry—or idolatry—in the Church as well. Did you know that it's possible for a man to be part of a Christian church and still be practicing idolatry? It's even possible for him to sit on a church board or stand behind the pulpit and be disobedient to the Lord and under a curse. God is no respecter of persons when it comes to sin and idolatry.

If you're a Mason, I understand how difficult it must be to believe that Freemasonry could be wrong if so many good men are involved in it. (By the way, you can put millions of good men—even pastors, deacons and elders—into the Lodge and it won't make the Lodge good.)

It really concerns me that so many ministers are members of the Lodge, standing behind the pulpit of their churches on Sunday and bowing at the altar of the Lodge on another night. Unfortunately, many good men unwittingly join the Lodge in complete ignorance because pastors and church leaders have failed to speak out on the dangers of secret societies. Speaking as a minister of the gospel, I must apologize for that and ask your forgiveness if no minister before now has shared with you the truth of Freemasonry.

REFORM, NOT RIDDANCE

Do you remember the story in the Old Testament of the prophet Hosea and his unfaithful wife, Gomer?[4] If it's an unfamiliar story to you, please read chapters 1 through 3 in the book of Hosea. It's a short book in the Old Testament, sandwiched between two other books of the Minor Prophets. In this story, God orders Hosea to take an adulterous woman as his wife. The union was a prophetic representation of God's relationship with the Israelites, who had committed spiritual adultery by worshiping Canaanite deities as the providers of grain, new wine and oil.[5]

The children of Hosea and Gomer were told to drive their unfaithful mother out of the house. But it was her reform, not her riddance, that was sought. Israel's alternative to destruction was to forsake her idols and return to the Lord. In spite of the harsh language with which the unavoidable judgment is announced, the major purpose of the book of Hosea is to pronounce God's compassion and love on Israel.[6] The story of Hosea and Gomer also serves as a reminder to the Church today of God's relentless love, even in the midst of idolatry.

Because God will not violate our will, He allows us to make our bad choices and go through hard times (see Heb. 12:4-11). Usually these hard times are small spankings, beneficial for midcourse adjustments. On occasion, when we are way off course, these spankings may be plentiful and with greater severity. At other times, when we're headed in the wrong direction entirely, punishment may come to a matter of "crushing." I've been there. It hurts! If you've been there, too, you know what I mean. But in all discipline, God has a purpose. It is our repentance and reform from sin and idolatry that He's after, not our riddance. You see, our loving heavenly Father really does miss us and He's jealous for our wholehearted return to Him.

A KING BOWS. . .AGAIN

In 2 Kings 21 you will find the story of King Manasseh, who bowed at the altars of the starry hosts—the sun, the moon and the stars. He engaged in all the idolatrous practices I've mentioned in earlier chapters.

> In both courts of the temple of the LORD, he built altars to all the starry hosts. He sacrificed his own son in the fire, practiced sorcery and divination, and consulted mediums and spiritists. He did much evil in the eyes of the LORD, provoking him to anger.[7]

I'm not relating this story to overwhelm you further or because you need another teaching on idolatry. Actually, this story provides hope. To find the happy ending of King Manasseh's story, you must turn to 2 Chronicles 33:12,13. You see, the king bowed again. Only this time, he bowed to the God of his fathers.

> In his distress he sought the favor of the LORD his God and humbled himself greatly before the God of his fathers. And when he prayed to him, the LORD was moved by his entreaty and listened to his plea; so he brought him back to Jerusalem and to his kingdom. Then Manasseh knew that the LORD is God.

Verses 15 and 16 then tell us:

> He got rid of the foreign gods and removed the image from the temple of the LORD, as well as all the altars he had built on the temple hill in Jerusalem; and he threw them out of the city. Then he restored the altar of the LORD and sacrificed fellowship offerings and thank offerings on it, and told Judah to serve the LORD, the God of Israel.

This account seems to be self-explanatory, but it may actually provide a model for getting free from Freemasonry. Let's look at the story again. Here is the Ron Campbell commentary on 2 Chronicles 33.

The seducing spirits behind the idols of Baal and Asherah enticed Manasseh into breaking covenant with God and entering into pacts with demons. Manasseh was on the wrong path, going astray and taking all Judah with him. This angered the Lord, so He "distressed" Manasseh. God showed His anger out of love, not to rid himself of Manasseh's presence. He wanted to humble and reform this wayward king.

In his distress, Manasseh recognized the truth of his idolatry, so he bowed once again, only this time it wasn't to the pagan deities who could provide nothing but death and destruction. This time he bowed to the God above all gods. He cried out, and the Lord was *moved by his entreaty.* I think God's ear was tuned to Manasseh's repentant cry! Why? Because it has always been God's heart "to seek and to save what was lost."[8] It has always been his heart, "not wanting anyone to perish, but everyone to come to repentance."[9]

Manasseh didn't stop with crying out to God. He set out to undo the damage he had done; he eradicated the pagan idols and altars from the land. He then went one step further by restoring the altar of the Lord and he sacrificed offerings upon it.

Do you know what I think? I think it was mandatory for Manasseh to first remove the pagan altars before he restored the altar of the Lord. I am convinced they cannot coexist. It is not a good thing for a man to kneel both at the altars of the Church and the altars of the Lodge.

Finally, Manasseh completed his repentance, reform and restoration by going back to encourage all of Judah, as well as those who had engaged in idolatry with him, to serve the God of Israel.

So what do you think? The model here is summarized as follows: A man committed idolatry. The hand of God was heavy upon him. He not only repented, but he reformed his ways. God heard his cry and saved him. The man no longer allowed the existence of the altars and idols; he threw them out of the city and out of his heart. (When I suggest we cast down idols and altars, I'm speaking metaphorically. While we have the authority to cast down the idols and altars of our hearts, we don't have the right to cast down physical structures owned by other individuals. Needless to say, this could land you in jail and usher in lawsuits.) Manasseh then restored the altar of the Lord and worshiped Him.

Finally, Manasseh went back to those he had influenced to engage in idolatry with him. He told them the truth and encouraged them to serve the God of Israel.

The Truth Will Make You Free!

That was Manasseh, and that was then. Now let's talk about the here and now.

If you are in Freemasonry, it is your loving Father's heart's desire that you be set free. If you are a Mason, please understand that no human being can set you free. You know what? *You* can't even make yourself free. It's true that you can physically leave the Lodge, but because the rituals and oaths you took involve spiritual matters, there is only One who can truly set you free. The price of any sin is too high, and nothing you or anyone else can do is sufficient to pay it. Only the Truth can make you free. This Truth is the person of Jesus Christ. He is not just another way to the Father, as Masonic philosophy would suggest. He is the *only* way, the *only* Truth and the *only* life.

Galatians 3:13 (*NASB*) tells us: "Christ redeemed us from the curse of the Law, having become a curse for us—for it is written, 'Cursed is everyone who hangs on a tree.' " In other words, there is no reason for anyone to remain under a curse. Jesus took on our curse so that we could have His righteousness. He provided the only remedy for sin, and His blood alone can remove the resultant curses of Freemasonry and idolatry. The choice is entirely yours; you can choose either blessings or curses, life or death.

Prayer of Release for Masons

If the conviction of the Holy Spirit has touched your heart, and you desire to repent and renounce your involvement in Freemasonry but are not sure how to do that, consider praying the following prayer. Remember that it must be prayed from a heart posture of humility and contrition.

If you would like someone to pray with you, I would suggest you contact your pastor or another trusted person who is a believer. However, if this seems unfavorable and you would like to contact our ministry for prayer and support, our address is listed at the back of this book. Now, let's pray the following prayer in faith and agreement:

Heavenly Father,

I come to You in the name of Jesus, Your *only* begotten Son. I recognize that my involvement in Freemasonry is idolatry, and I understand from Scripture that idolatry is sin.

I confess that I was deceived and sought out a light other than the true Light of Your Son, Jesus. I repent that I allowed a blindfold to be placed over my eyes and for declaring that I was in darkness. I now confess that Jesus is the Light, the *only* Light.

I repent for allowing a cable tow to be placed around my body, signifying my covenant to someone other than You. I repent for the covenants that I made, whether knowingly or otherwise, with the gods of the Lodge. I now confess my allegiance to You and You alone.

I repent for bowing my knees and uttering abominable oaths at the altar of Freemasonry, such as having my throat cut from ear to ear, my heart torn out and my body cut in two. I will never again bow my knee at the altars of strange gods. I thank You now for the atoning blood of Jesus Christ that cleanses me from all this unrighteousness.

I repent for the sin of engaging in a counterfeit death, burial and resurrection of a pagan deity in the third degree. I'm sorry I allowed myself to be resurrected into anything other than the resurrection power of Jesus Christ. Please forgive me. I now declare there is no resurrection outside of Jesus Christ; He alone is the way, the truth and the life.

I repent further for the sinful rites and oaths taken during all the other Masonic degrees in which I participated.

Father, please forgive me for leading others to the altars of Freemasonry and assisting them in abominable acts. I pray that they will also find the truth in Jesus Christ that will set them free.

I confess that my sin of idolatry has not only affected me, but it has also opened the door to curses on my family. I repent for this sin and ask that You would remove the reproach of my sin from my children and all subsequent generations. Father, please set them free! I renounce all the curses listed in Deuteronomy 28 that are associated with idolatry. I now ask for Your grace and mercy to replace those curses with the blessings You desire for me and my family.

Heavenly Father, I believe in my heart and confess with my mouth that You have forgiven me through the blood—the death, resurrection and ascension of Christ to Your right hand. I also declare that those whom You set free are free indeed. Therefore, I and my family for generations to come are now free from the bondage of Freemasonry.

I pray now, Father, that You would build a hedge of protection around me and my family. Protect us and all that You have entrusted to us. I pray for abundant grace and strength to resist Satan, the roaring lion who seeks whom he may devour. I declare that the blood of Jesus covers my family and me.

Thank You so much, and I pray all this in the name of Jesus, Your Son and our Savior. Amen.

You may choose to continue your prayer of repentance and renunciation by praying the prayer of release in the final chapter of this book. May God abundantly bless you in your newfound freedom in Him!

Notes

1. Albert Pike, *Morals and Dogma of the Ancient and Accepted Scottish Rite of Freemasonry* (Richmond, Va.: L. H. Jenkins, 1947), pp. 104, 105, from a section of instruction to candidates of the Third Degree.
2. This gentleman chooses to remain anonymous.

3. Deuteronomy 11:26-28.
4. Hosea, chapters 1—3.
5. See Hosea 2:8.
6. The *NIV Study Bible,* on the theme and message of Hosea, p. 1322.
7. 2 Kings 21:5,6.
8. Luke 19:10.
9. 2 Peter 3:9.

CHAPTER NINE

Understanding Generational Curses

You shall not make for yourself an idol in the form of anything in heaven above....You shall not bow down to them or worship them; for I, the Lord your God, am a jealous God, punishing the children for the sin of the fathers to the third and fourth generation of those who hate me.

GOD, THROUGH MOSES, EXODUS 20:4,5

It is time to consider Masonry's lingering effects on friends and family members. Have the secret oaths and esoteric rituals acted out by Masons behind the closed doors of the Lodge opened other doors that may not be as easily recognized? That is, have they opened entry points for curses that now oppress their loved ones? Yes!

Most Masons do not understand the seriousness of the evil they have embraced or they would not knowingly engage in pagan rituals and all they entail—the breaking of God's commandments and the ripping away of the protective spiritual covering over our loved ones—which leaves them vulnerable to Satan's deadly attacks, even for generations to come. Yet here lies the power and attraction of evil: It often seems good but always draws us away from God.

Ignorance, however, does not diminish or negate the damage done by good men engaging in idolatrous practices. Through their disobedience to God's Word, the door is opened for curses to visit to the third and fourth generation. These doorways, or entry points, allow the enemy to wreak havoc upon families. In a moment we will learn how to close these doors; but before we can effectively deal with generational curses that oppress our loved ones, we must first understand what curses are, where they originate and how they operate.

There are a number of good books that address the subject of curses. One of my favorites is a small power-packed book written by Frank and Ida Mae Hammond, titled *The Breaking of Curses*. I give credit to the Hammonds for much of the material in this chapter.

What Is a Curse?

I was raised in a conservative evangelical denominational church (this is not a bad thing!), which seldom taught about curses. When my charismatic friends began to talk to me about curses, particularly generational curses, I was somewhat skeptical, to say the least. When I first heard the word "curse," it conjured visions of the cackling Wicked Witch of the West in the classic movie *The Wizard of Oz*, as she breathed her fiery curses at Dorothy and her dog, Toto. Fortunately, a curse means something quite different to me today than it did even a few years ago.

The word "curse" evokes a variety of responses in different individuals. To many people, curses are the use of foul language or profanity. Others think of curses as nothing more than the stuff of fairy tales, with witches casting spells and hexes and turning handsome princes into ugly toads. Then there are some who see a demon behind every bush. They blame curses for every negative incident or problem they have ever encountered. At the other end of the spectrum are those who are so afraid of becoming curse conscious (putting overemphasis on them) that they become curse *un*conscious. And finally, there are those who won't even consider the possibility. You can almost hear this person say, "Curses are from the dark ages; we're so much smarter today."

Positioned somewhere on the continuum between these two extremes—those who blame curses for anything negative and those who refuse to believe curses exist—are those who are at least open to the possibilities of demons and curses, yet they remain guarded. They've heard some whacked-out stories and teaching and have questions regarding the biblical basis for curses. They want more evidence to form a healthy conclusion. I trust the final two chapters of this book will ease much of the confusion and fear relating to generational curses, particularly curses brought about by unsuspecting loved ones who have bowed their knees at the altar of Freemasonry.

When I learned from the Hammonds' book that the word "curse" is actually mentioned in some form or another over 230 times in the Bible, I could hardly believe it. There are six different words in Hebrew for the word "curse." In Greek, this word has three translations. The Hebrew word *arar* is actually the most common and means "to utter a wish of evil against; to call for mischief or injury to fall upon, or to bind with a spell." *Cherem* is also translated "curse" and means "things designated for God or earmarked for destruction." The Old Testament ideas of curses and cursing passed into the Greek New Testament in the use of seven words, the most important of which is *anathema*.[1]

The curses we will discuss in these final chapters are not the kind actively and intentionally "called down" by people to bring evil, mischief or injury upon others. The curses we will consider are those brought about as a sentence or divine judgment for disobedience to God's commands. These curses are the opposite of the covenantal blessings God desires for His children. If you carefully read Deuteronomy 27—28, you will discover that the curses listed are the repercussions of a person violating his relationship with God. Simply stated, God says, "If you obey me, you can expect blessings; if you disobey me, you can expect curses."

The Reality of Curses

Are curses real? They were real in the Old Testament. If Hiel of Bethel were still alive today, he would tell you that curses are real. His disobedience to the Lord led to his punishment, which was prophetically pronounced by Joshua against anyone who rebuilt the city of Jericho. Hiel's disobedience cost him the lives of two of his children. You can read of Hiel's judgment in Joshua 6:26 and 1 Kings 16:34.

Curses were real in the New Testament, too. Ask Jesus. Galatians 3:13 (*NASB*) tells us: "Christ redeemed us from the curse of the Law, having become a curse for us—for it is written, 'Cursed is everyone who hangs on a tree.' " In other words, there is no reason for anyone to remain under a curse; Jesus provided the remedy when He took the curse of breaking God's law upon Himself, once for all, to reconcile us back to God (see Heb. 9:26-28).

Are curses real today? Ask Craig and Bev Osborne, discipled through Cleansing Stream Ministries (a healing and deliverance ministry based in California under the umbrella of Jack Hayford

and The Church on the Way). During a retreat, a partially para-
lyzed woman came to Bev and asked if Freemasonry had anything to do with sickness. Bev prayed a simple prayer, breaking
the curse of Freemasonry, and the woman was instantly and
completely healed. The woman later carried her leg brace in her
hand, weeping and proclaiming her healing. I'm certain that if
the truth were known, there are thousands of testimonies like
Bev's, resulting from Masons—and others who have been put
under consequential curses—getting free.

GOD LINKS THE RESPONSIBILITY OF
WORSHIPING HIM ALONE TO THE BLESSING
OR CURSING OF OUR CHILDREN
THROUGH OUR ACTIONS.

Many scriptural references allude to the reality of curses.
Here are just a few:

- You shall have no other gods before me. You shall not
  make yourself an idol in the form of anything in heav-
  en above or on the earth beneath or in the waters below.
  You shall not bow down to them or worship them. For
  I, the LORD your God, am a jealous God, punishing the

children for the sin of the fathers to the third and
fourth generation of those who hate me, but showing
love to a thousand generations of those who love me
and keep my commandments (Exod. 20:3-6).

In this passage, God links the responsibility of worshiping
Him alone to the blessing or cursing of our children through
our actions. The word "father" in the Bible often alludes to
"ancestors."

- Do not blaspheme God or curse the ruler of your people
  (Exod. 22:28).

While there is room for constructive criticism of our civil
authorities, we are cautioned to avoid cursing them. Instead of
cursing those in authority over us, we are to pray for them (see 1
Tim. 2:1,2).

- The LORD, the LORD, the compassionate and gracious
  God, slow to anger, abounding in love and faithfulness,
  maintaining love to thousands, and forgiving wickedness, rebellion and sin. Yet he does not leave the guilty
  unpunished; he punishes the children and their children for the sin of the fathers to the third and fourth
  generation (Exod. 34:6,7).

Here, God gives His people a strong warning about what will
happen if they go astray and do not repent.

- The tongue has the power of life and death, and those
  who love it will eat its fruit (Prov. 18:21).

This Scripture suggests that we have the power within us to speak forth blessings and life, or curses and death.

The Sources of Curses

Assuming then that curses are real, how do curses originate? Are they simply spoken into existence? Do they come mostly from Satan, witches and warlocks? Let's identify the sources of curses.[2]

- First, it may surprise you to find that curses sometimes come from God Himself, as we just read in Exodus 20:5. Although they may originate from the Lord, they are activated through our own disobedience. They are consequences of our sin and are often used by the Lord to "distress" us as incentive to come back to Him. Remember, it is our reform, not our riddance, that God is after.
- It is no secret that the servants of Satan often place curses and hexes on individuals and objects.
- God's servants, surprisingly enough, also sometimes declare curses. Joshua 6:26 informs us: "Joshua pronounced this solemn oath: 'Cursed before the LORD is the man who undertakes to rebuild this city, Jericho.' "
- In 1 Corinthians 16:22, we find Paul declaring a curse on those who do not love the Lord. This curse was not based on an oath that Jesus forbids; it was based on God as witness to the unbeliever's essential lack of love and obedience to God.[3] Paul also declares in Galatians 1:8,9 that anyone who preaches a gospel other than that which he presented should be eternally condemned.
- Curses can also be self-imposed. For example, in Genesis 27:13, Rebekah said: "Let [your] curse fall on

me." Then in Matthew 27:25, the Jews who were agitating for Jesus' death said: "Let his blood be on us and on our children!" Masons and anyone else making vows to anyone other than the one true God also impose curses upon themselves. You might recall from an earlier chapter that our friend John Laurens declared:

All this, I, [John Laurens], most solemnly, sincerely promise and swear, with a firm and steady resolution, to perform the same, without any hesitation, mental reservation, or secret evasion of mind whatever, binding myself, under no less penalty than that of having my body severed in two, my bowels taken from thence and burned to ashes, the ashes scattered before the four winds of heaven, that no more remembrance might be had of so vile and wicked a wretch as I would be, would I ever, knowingly, violate this my Master Mason's obligation. So help me God, and keep me steadfast in the due performance of the same.[4]

I'm convinced that many Masons are cursed with a subconscious fear of death as a result of taking these appalling oaths.

- Finally, there are curses that the Hammonds refer to as "Authority-Engendered Curses." It is these types of curses that are activated upon a family when a man bows his knee at a Masonic altar.

Authority-Engendered Curses

According to the Bible, all of us live under authority of various kinds, and most of us eventually will have authority over some. But all authority ultimately derives from God.

The simple concept of Authority-Engendered Curses is this: "All authority is vested in God, and God has chosen to exercise His rule through the delegation of authority to men and angels....Delegated authorities include kings and all civil magistrates, husbands, parents and church leaders. Not only does an authority bless or curse, with words, those who are submitted to him, *but he blesses or curses them through his righteousness or the lack thereof* "[5](italics mine).

For a scriptural account of how curses are activated over an entire nation or geographic region under the authority of a king or civil magistrate, we need only look at the lives of Saul and David. Saul disobeyed the Lord by putting the Gibeonites to death, and the land was cursed with a famine for three successive years.[6] David took a census of his fighting men and it so displeased the Lord that a plague broke out and killed 70,000 men before it could be stopped.[7] In these two instances we can see that although those under the authority of the kings didn't commit the sins, they were greatly affected by the consequential curses of those sins.

The authority structure we want to focus on here as it relates to curses is the family, particularly the role of the father. Take the example of a father trying to be the priest of the home. He is the "spiritual covering" and provides an umbrella of spiritual protection over his family and loved ones. When the father is disobedient and sins, the umbrella of protection is ripped. Through that rip, the adversary is then able to saturate with oppressive storms in the form of demonic curses those under this father's authority and protection. According to Ephesians 4:27, when we sin, we open the door, or provide an entry point, for Satan. Essentially, we give him permission to oppress our loved ones. Through the unrighteousness of one in spiritual authority over others, curses can now visit to the third and fourth generation.

Grasping the concept of authority-engendered curses is sometimes difficult. It raises many questions. For example, Why would a good God allow evil curses to fall upon those who are innocent of the sin? And what about that famous passage in Ezekiel 18, which establishes that each individual is responsible before God for his own actions? Doesn't this Scripture say that the sons were not to be punished for the sins of their fathers and vice versa? And that the person who sinned would die and the person who did right would live?

These questions are easily asked, yet difficult to answer, particularly because the answers seem to challenge the very character and nature of God. Before I address the Ezekiel 18 passage as it relates to generational curses, let me first explain what I mean by "generational curse."

GENERATIONAL CURSES

Some scholars suggest that a generation may include a span of 40 years; others would suggest it is as much as 100 years. When I refer to a generation, I'm using a dictionary definition to mean "the average interval of time between the birth of the parents and the birth of their offspring." In other words, my generation would include the offspring of my parents; that is, my brothers, sisters and me. The next generation would include my children and their cousins, or the grandchildren of my parents, and so on.

Exodus 34 tells us that curses pass to the third and fourth generations. Suppose a man commits the sin of idolatry. Further suppose that he and each of his descendants for four generations have three children each. This adds up to 40 descendants who will come under the curse of that one man's iniquity.

Each person, by going backward on this generational chart, has 2 parents, 4 grandparents, 8 great-grandparents and 16 great-great grandparents. This provides a total of 30 ancestors from whom curses could possibly have filtered down upon us.[8] These are the curses that I call generational curses, and it's not unlikely that many of us are experiencing them rather than blessings because one or more of these ancestors have unwisely opened the door to our adversary.

Now, back to the Ezekiel 18 passage. The teaching in this passage regarding a person's individual responsibility for his actions does not negate generational punishment for sins committed by a family member or ancestor. In fact, it is an individual's ability to choose blessing or cursing that links this passage to the concept of generational curses. Here's what I mean.

The Bible tells us that none of us is totally innocent of sin. All humans are affected by the Fall described in Genesis 3 and not one of us has been able to extricate him- or herself from the vicious cycle of sin and death (i.e., the curse of the law). But God presents all of us with the choice between spiritual life (repentance and forgiveness through Jesus Christ) and spiritual death (continuing in sin and separation from God). Both blessings and cursings are conditional upon our heart attitude toward God.

If we choose life and are cleansed from the guilt and stain and shame of sin, through the blood of Christ, we can pass on spiritual blessings to our children and their children "to a thousand generations of those who love him" (Deut. 7:9), and we can hope for eventual wholeness in the resurrection (see Rev. 22:3).

These blessings are passed down from generation to generation but depend upon each generation individually responding to God through repentance from sin and seeking to honor God. However, if we do not repent and we continue in rebellion against God and His Son, in effect we are choosing spiritual death and subjecting our children to the ravages of the enemy of their souls. According to Exodus 20:3-5, sin can (and is) passed from generation to generation unless someone breaks the cycle through repentance, loving God and allowing his or her life to be transformed by Him.

No one's spiritual fate is sealed by another's decision—all of us are individually responsible for our own lives and are accountable to God. If any of the children of those who turn away from God repent from their wickedness and turn back to God, God will have mercy on them, forgiving them their sins, removing the curses upon them through the blood of Christ, filling them with the same Holy Spirit and making the same promises of "love to a thousand generations of those who love me" (Exod. 20:6).

In other words, Christ enables all of us who have failed to love God with all our hearts and our neighbor as ourselves—that means all of us (see Matt. 22:37-39; Rom. 3:23; 6:23)—to acknowledge individually the responsibility for our sin, to repent and to be transformed by Christ. But we are still part of the human race and part of our own generational line.

Putting our trust in Christ takes care of the main curse that plagues us, the curse of the law. But that act does not automatically discount the possibility of other kinds of curses, including generational curses, as if we could remove ourselves from the human race without any connection to previous and coming generations.

On the contrary, just as God has provided us a means of escape from the penalty and punishment of sin through Christ's blood shed for us on the Cross, so God has also provided us a means of cleansing from all the curses which might be upon us in our generational lines, whether we are aware of them or not, through the washing of rebirth and renewal through the Holy Spirit (see Titus 3:5).

Symptoms of Curses

How can you recognize if a curse is active in your life or that of a friend or family member? You may begin by comparing your life to the blessings God has promised. As you take inventory, do your findings measure up to those blessings mentioned in Deuteronomy 28:1-14? The following are earmarks of a blessed life:

Are you "set on high" by God, a lender and not a borrower, the head and not the tail? Is your life characterized by fruitfulness? Do you prosper—coming and going? Are you free from the harassment of enemies—both natural and spiritual? Is your life a success? Is your relation to God gratifying; are you recognizing and fulfilling His purposes?[9]

If you or your loved ones are not enjoying the blessings, then it's possible that you are suffering the curses. In a moment, we'll look at some of the more common symptoms of these curses. Before we do, please note a couple of important points. First, we must acknowledge that just because someone is experiencing difficulties doesn't necessarily prove that he or she is under a curse. For example, look at the life of Job. Job was a righteous man, yet he experienced extreme difficulty. If he were alive today, I'm sure many of us would try to break curses off him.

Secondly, if we are experiencing the symptoms of curses, our forefathers may not be the ones who opened the doors to them. It's possible they are open as a direct result of *our own* sin and disobedience. We must be cautious and steer clear of the blaming game. Not accepting responsibility for our own actions will always hinder our freedom!

For several years now, I've observed the possible effects of Freemasonry on families, cities and nations. At first I was skeptical when others suggested that certain negative fruit in individuals' lives stemmed from roots planted deeply in the contaminated soil of Freemasonry. As my understanding of Freemasonry grew, so did my openness to the cause-and-effect relationship between the secret oaths and rituals of Masonry and the subsequent active curses that seemed to fall upon Masons' families.

The following symptoms are in no way specific only to Masons or those in the generational lines of Masons. It is my general impression and that of my colleagues that the people who are tied to Freemasonry tend to have a lot of these kinds of problems.

Poverty. When I refer to poverty, I do not mean a season of financial stress or difficulty. Rather, I'm referring more to perpetual financial insufficiency. Incidentally, you've probably noticed as I have that many Masons appear to be successful businessmen and have wealth. Please understand that it is possible to have great wealth and still have a poverty spirit. The focus of a person with a poverty spirit is usually not on what he has but on what he lacks. He is fearful of not having enough and frequently becomes a nongiver.

Barrenness and impotency, together with miscarriages and female-related problems. Darla and I have numerous friends who can't conceive, and the last thing we would ever do is heap coals of condemnation upon their already aching hearts. I'm not a doctor, and I don't understand all the complicated issues related to barrenness, but Scripture clearly states that barrenness can be related to curses activated by the sins of forefathers, particularly if that sin is idolatry (see Deut. 28:18).

Breakdown of family relationships, including divorce. This shouldn't surprise us when we consider that we're dealing with a covenant-breaking seducing spirit as old as history itself.

Pestilence. In the Old Testament, pestilences usually came in the form of insects that devoured the crops. Though the curse of pestilence may operate similarly today, I think the definition may expand to include the devouring of any intended "harvest."

Chronic sickness. This means repeated or lengthy illnesses. Some of these illnesses include but are not limited to heart problems, cancer, respiratory problems, allergies, throat ailments, strokes and attacks on the mind.

Defeat and failure. This symptom is summed up best by the words of Derek Prince in his excellent book *Blessing or Curse*:

> A curse could also be likened to a long evil arm stretched out from the past. It rests upon you with a dark, oppressive force that inhibits the full expression of your personality. You never feel completely free to be yourself. You sense you have potential within you that is never fully developed. You always expect more of yourself than you are able to achieve.[10]

Mental illness, torment and confusion. Occasionally the mental confusion is so strong that those involved in the deliverance tell of experiencing confusion and dizziness as well.

Perpetual traumas. This involves moving from one conflict to the next—continually "putting out fires." This person lives in a reactive rather than proactive state.

Proneness to accidents. Recently a parent mentioned to me that she often wondered if she should take out an extra insurance policy on one of her sons because he was so prone to accidents.

Emotional hardness. This is most prevalent in men, particularly as it relates to outward expression of affection toward their children.

Having a "religious spirit," or controlling spirit. This symptom manifests as a form of godliness but denies the power. In other words, it is religious and loves religion but does not love the Spirit of God. Thus, it attempts to rebel and control rather than submit to the Holy Spirit.

Premature and violent death. This is a tough one, but it comes across my desk and is mentioned by conference attendees much too often to ignore. My colleagues and I admit that while proof is impossible as it relates to individual cases, there remains a high probability of premature death as it relates to idolatry.

Although I realize that not all premature and violent deaths are the result of curses, I include the following account by Noel and Phyllis Gibson from their book *Evicting Demonic Intruders*, not because it is proof positive of the consequences of active Masonic curses, but because it is not uncommon to many of the stories shared with me by hurting individuals.

> During a deliverance seminar, a participant submitted a question which surely provokes some thought. It was, "Freemasonry—could the following be its effects?"

- My father was a Freemason—also a Christian. I'm not sure he's ever renounced it, but I don't think he goes to any meetings now.
- My brother, a missionary, was martyred in 1962 (age 26).
- My sister died of cancer at age 18 in 1964.
- My niece, age 20, was killed in a motor accident in 1980.
- My mother had a stroke in 1975.
- My brother had a stroke in 1985 (age 46).[11]

Spiritual hindrances and spiritual apathy. It's as though something is hindering a person from attaining a deep intimacy with the Lord. As a result, this individual's spiritual discernment is also impaired.

Doubt, skepticism, unbelief and mockery. This symptom often parades as intellectualism.

Pride and arrogance. There is an obvious lack of grace in this person's life. In fact, there seems to be a resistance from the Lord. It is a manifestation of the Scripture in James 4:6: "God opposes the proud but gives grace to the humble."

THE OATH, THE BLINDFOLD AND THE CABLE TOW

In a moment we will look at the curses listed in Deuteronomy 28. Before we do, there are a few symptoms of Masonic curses that demand special attention. They are directly linked to the Masonic oaths that are related to the blindfold and cable tow the candidate wears in the initiation ritual. The blindfold points to a profound spiritual deception. If you have ever ministered to a friend or relative who is in the Lodge, you may have noticed that he appears to be under great deception. While you're questioning how this person could be so deceived, he's asking the same about you. Have you ever wondered how a man could progress through all of the degrees of Masonry and still not see the truth? I believe a partial answer to that question is found in the ritual of the first degree.

You might remember that after our friend John Laurens was escorted to the Lodge door blindfolded, his guide verbally declared that Laurens "has long been in darkness, and now seeks to be brought to light."[12] I believe that when *he allowed* the blindfold to be placed around his eyes, together with the *verbal declaration* that he was yet in the darkness, he opened the door to deception. He was then able to progress through the various degrees without ever discerning the truth of Freemasonry.

The second symptom is actually a group of symptoms involving physical ailments that could be directly linked to the oaths and cable tow. Remember that the cable tow is the cord of three strands wrapped around the candidate's throat, chest and stomach as he progresses through the first three degrees. At the same time the candidate declares that if he divulges Masonic secrets he will have his throat cut from ear to ear, his heart torn out, be disemboweled and have his body cut in two. As the candidate voluntarily engages in this bizarre ritual, he opens the door to infirmities such as throat disorders, heart and respiratory diseases and chronic stomach problems.

The cable tow around the candidate may also help explain why it is so difficult to get Masons free from Freemasonry. Albert Mackey tells us:

In its inception, the cable tow seems to have been used only as a physical means of controlling the candidate....But in the Second and Third degrees a more modern symbolism has been introduced, and the cable tow is in these grades supposed to symbolize the covenant by which all Masons are tied.[13]

Mackey further informs us that according to the ancient laws of Freemasonry, "every brother must attend his Lodge if he is within the length of his cable tow."[14] It's as though an invisible cord of bondage is wrapped around a Mason, keeping him ever mindful of his obligations to the Craft.

The final symptom of possible curses associated with Freemasonry is the unhealthy fear of death. It doesn't take a rocket scientist to see how this is possible. After all, the candidate was led blindfolded into the Lodge, was beaten up by his peers, was symbolically killed by the same, was buried in rubbish and finally played out an impossible resurrection. In a real sense, he made a covenant with the grave. The residue that remains is fear.

THE DEUTERONOMY "CURSE LIST"

As we have seen in Deuteronomy 28, there is a blessing list and a curse list. An optimist would probably spend more time meditating on the blessing list, while the pessimist would occupy his time on the curses. I apologize to you optimists, but we need to look at the curse list for a few moments.

It is interesting to note that the Lord transitions from the blessings to the curses with this statement: "Do not turn aside from any of the commands I give you today, to the right or to the left, *following other gods and serving them*"[15] (italics mine). I think it's significant that idolatry is usually prioritized at the top of God's list, particularly as it relates to judgments and curses.[16]

When we compare our previous list of curse symptoms to the curses listed in Deuteronomy 28, we move from the realm of *possibilities* to *probabilities*. If it's mentioned in the Bible, it kind of makes it seem more believable, doesn't it? Let's look at Deuteronomy 28:15-68; it is a lengthy portion of Scripture, so allow me to highlight the curses only. They include the following:

> Famine, barrenness on the fruit of your womb, confusion and rebuke, plagues, diseases and physical infirmities, bronze skies overhead and iron ground beneath your feet, defeat, madness, confusion of mind, blindness, oppression and being robbed, sowing but not reaping, separation between parents and children, scorn, humiliation and ridicule, bondage, pestilences, being a borrower and not a lender, sinking lower and not rising higher, being the tail and not the head, poverty, hunger and thirst, nakedness, military defeat, lack of familial compassion, prolonged disasters, lingering illnesses, being uprooted from your promised

possession, forced idolatry, constant suspense, dread day and night.

It's a disheartening list. However, you can be encouraged that because of God's great love and grace, the story doesn't end here. Stay with me for the final chapter and we will move toward victory over these deadly curses. With a foundational understanding of generational curses, it is now time to learn about the authority we have to break them. It's now time to learn how we can get free from Freemasonry.

Notes

1. See Wilhelm Mundel, Hugo Aust, Dietrich Müller and Theo Sorg's articles under "Curse, Insult, Fool" in *The New International Dictionary of New Testament Theology*, Vol. 1 (Grand Rapids: Eerdmans, 1967 in German, 1986 translated into English), pp. 413-418. For the other Hebrew and Greek words which translate "curse," "cursed" or "cursing," see Robert Young, *Young's Analytical Concordance to the Bible* (Grand Rapids: Eerdmans, 1955, reprinted 1983).
2. Taken from a brochure distributed by Fruitful Vine.
3. *The NIV Study Bible*, p. 1760.
4. Malcolm C. Duncan, *Duncan's Ritual of Freemasonry* (New York: David McKay Company, n.d.), p. 96.
5. Frank and Ida Mae Hammond, *The Breaking of Curses* (Plainview, Tex.: Impact Books, 1993), p. 52.
6. See 2 Samuel 21:1.
7. See 1 Chronicles 21:1-17.
8. This concept was taken from Hammond, *The Breaking of Curses*, p. 10.
9. Ibid., p. 17.
10. Derek Prince, *Blessing or Curse: You Can Choose* (Grand Rapids, Mich.: Chosen Books, 1990), p. 17.
11. Noel and Phyllis Gibson, *Evicting Demonic Intruders* (West Sussex, England: New Wine Press, 1993), p. 130.
12. Duncan, *Duncan's Ritual of Freemasonry*, p. 29.
13. Albert Mackey, *An Enclyclopedia of Freemasonry*, Vol. 1 (New York: The Masonic History Company, 1915), p. 126.
14. Ibid.
15. Deuteronomy 28:14.
16. See Exodus 20:3,4.

CHAPTER TEN

FREEDOM FROM THE CURSES OF FREEMASONRY

In its first inception, the cable tow seems to have been used only as a physical means of controlling the candidate....In the Second and Third degrees a more modern symbolism has been introduced, and the cable tow in these grades is supposed to symbolize the covenant by which all Masons are tied.[1]

ALBERT MACKEY,
AN ENCYCLOPEDIA OF FREEMASONRY

It is for freedom that Christ has set us free. Stand firm, then, and do not let yourselves be burdened again by a yoke of slavery.

APOSTLE PAUL, GALATIANS 5:1

THE THREE RS OF GETTING FREE

By now you recognize the fourfold purpose of this book: (1) to share my concern with those not yet in the Lodge, in hopes they never get involved, (2) to educate Masons and their loved ones about the truth of Freemasonry, (3) to get Masons free from the Lodge and (4) to assist families of Masons to get free from the generational curses of Freemasonry.

Chapter 8 was geared toward men yet trapped in the Lodge, and chapter 9 to understanding how generational curses are passed on to their loved ones. Now let's get free!

At the risk of oversimplifying this journey to freedom, I would like to introduce the three Rs that will get you there. The first R is to *recognize* that Freemasonry is idolatry and idolatry is sin. The second R is to *repent* for that sin. The third R is to formally *renounce*, or reject, the oaths and curses of Freemasonry.

RECOGNIZE THE SIN OF IDOLATRY

My research reveals that Freemasonry is idolatry. The Bible is absolutely clear that idolatry is sin. The dictionary defines idolatry as "excessive devotion or the worship of idols." When most Americans hear the word "idolatry," they think of excessive devotion to or misplaced priorities involving worldly wealth.

While excessive devotion to anything could be viewed as idolatry, I'm referring to bestowing allegiance and worship on a supernatural being other than God. This is blatant idolatry and it is in this sense that I use the term as it relates to Freemasonry.

REPENT FOR THE SIN OF IDOLATRY

After we recognize Freemasonry as idolatry, we must repent for that sin. Repentance is more than mere words. It is possible to say "I'm sorry" and not be truly repentant. Repentance is also more than a physical posture. True repentance is an issue of the heart and demands a heart posture of contrition. When you repent for the sin of idolatry, let it be from your heart, because I assure you this sin touches the heart of God.

IDENTIFICATIONAL REPENTANCE

As we talk about repentance, we must familiarize ourselves with a term that is relatively new to the Body of Christ. This term is "identificational repentance." While the term is new, the practice or concept is nearly as old as history itself. I like how Dr. Peter Wagner introduces it in a little brochure titled *The Power to Change the Past*:

> In order to understand [identificational repentance], let's go from the known to the unknown. Most of us have been well trained to understand personal repentance. We know that sin can and does invade our personal lives. When it does, it has devastating effects not only on us but on others around us. And we know what to do about it when it happens:
>
> · Identify the sin specifically.
> · Sincerely confess the sin and ask God to forgive it.
> · Know that God is faithful and just to forgive us our sins.
> · Once forgiven, walk in obedience from that point onward.[2]

We are familiar with our own need for individual repentance of our sin, but the Bible also talks about the "iniquity of the father"[3] that passes from generation to generation. Dr. Wagner differentiates iniquity from sin: "Technically speaking, sin can be understood as the initial act, while iniquity is the effect that the sin has exercised on the subsequent generations."[4] It is not only possible to see how the iniquities of our forefathers visit us personally, but also as a nation. In the case of the origin of the United States, for example, many of the founders of our country were Masons and committed the sin of idolatry, binding themselves to curses. The iniquity, or effect, of that sin still visits us.

Time alone does not heal the iniquity of the fathers. In fact, Dr. Wagner suggests that if the sin is not remitted, the iniquity more frequently than not can become worse in each succeeding generation. The only persons who can confess the sin and put it under the blood of Jesus Christ are those who are alive today. Even though they did not commit the sin themselves, they can choose to identify with it, thus the term "identificational repentance."[5]

I know this is uncharted water for some and you may feel a little uneasy about identificational repentance. However, before I validate this concept through Scripture, for the sake of clarification let me give context to what I'm saying. It might help put you at ease.

Let's say that your grandfather was a Mason and is now deceased. Because he went through all the rituals we have discussed, the iniquity—or effects—of his sin would visit you. You could be oppressed by curses as a result of sins you did not commit. (Remember authority-engendered curses?) Sounds harsh, doesn't it. You finally grasp the truth of the matter and decide you have had enough. You're sick and tired of poverty, sickness, confusion and lack of destiny and purpose. There's a spiritual door open in your family's history and it must be closed. There's sin in the camp and someone must take the responsibility and repent. However, your grandfather has since passed on and can't repent. What should you do?

First, understand that you can't repent *for* the sins of your grandfather, for Scripture is clear: "The soul who sins is the one who will die."[6] In other words, you cannot stand in as an intercessor and repent for his sins for *his* sake. This is impossible and is *not* what I mean by identificational repentance.

Second, understand that you can and should repent *because* of the sins of your grandfather and *because* his sins still affect you in the form of curses. This is more than mere semantics, so please stay with me. Here's how it works. As a grandchild you have an identity with his family. As a family member you may also choose to identify with his sin, confess it and put it under the blood of Jesus. Your cry to the Lord may go something like this:

> Heavenly Father, thank You so much for Your love to me and my family. Thank You that You have a hope and a purpose for us.
>
> Father, You've revealed to me that there is sin in my family. I confess my sin and the sin of my fathers, for we have embraced the gods of Egypt, Greece and Rome. Through the blood of Your Son and our Savior, Jesus Christ, please forgive us and remove the reproach from our lives.

We have three biblical examples of how this is done:

> Daniel said, "I was...confessing my sin and the sin of my people" (Dan. 9:20).

> Nehemiah said that both his father's house and he had sinned (see Neh. 1:6).

> Jeremiah said, "O LORD, we acknowledge our wickedness and the guilt of our fathers; we have indeed sinned against you" (Jer. 14:20).

Identificational repentance can be a very powerful tool in getting free from the generational curses, whether of Freemasonry or any other kind of generational curse.

RENOUNCE THE SIN OF IDOLATRY
To renounce simply means to give up, or reject, especially by formal announcement or declaration. When praying with Masons

or their families, Darla and I have discovered that there seems to be additional power and anointing when an individual *verbally* declares his renunciation of Masonic bondage and curses. There is power in the spoken word. Scripture informs us that we have the power to speak life or speak death (see Prov. 18:21).

Masons verbally speak their oaths. Consequently, their spoken words activate the curses and iniquities that visit to the third and fourth generations. In a similar way, we should verbally renounce and reject the sin of idolatry. *Speak out,* that the powers of the occult may hear that they no longer have a hold on your life and the lives of your children and their children's children. "Christ in you, the hope of glory" (Col. 1:27) has become the curse for you and has given you the power to break the cycle of bondage that has existed for generations (see Col. 1:27; Gal. 3:13,14).

WHEN A MASON OR HIS LOVED ONES RECOGNIZE, REPENT AND RENOUNCE THE WICKED OATHS AND CURSES OF FREEMASONRY, THEY ARE IN A SENSE UNDOING, OR UNRAVELING, THE ADVERSARY'S PLANS FOR THEIR LIVES.

SYMBOLIC, OR PROPHETIC, ACTS

Symbolic acts, or what some would call prophetic acts, make a statement. They have nothing to do with rituals or manipulating the spirit world. These acts simply declare, or announce, to those watching—not only in the physical but also in the spirit realm—that we are serious about our freedom. I believe these symbolic, or prophetic, acts often parallel that which is happening in the spirit. For example, when a Mason allows a blindfold to be placed around his eyes and then declares that he is in the darkness, he is at that moment acting out what is happening in the spirit. He has not entered the light promised by the Lodge; he has entered darkness and spiritual blindness.

Likewise, when a Mason allows an actual cable tow to be placed around his neck, chest and waist as a symbol of his new covenant with the Lodge, he is entering into a spiritual covenant with, or bondage to, the strange deity of Freemasonry.

When a Mason or his loved ones recognize, repent and renounce the wicked oaths and curses of Freemasonry, they are in a sense undoing, or unraveling, the adversary's plans for their lives. Therefore, it only seems right and good to declare this freedom to the prince of darkness by symbolically removing the blindfold and cable tow.

Darla and I ask those to whom we're ministering to act out the removal of these vestiges of bondage as though they physically exist on their eyes and necks. As they do this, the anointing to break the yoke comes down on most individuals, and the Holy Spirit seems to confirm that this prophetic act is paralleling their freedom from the generational curses of Freemasonry.

DESTROY MASONIC REGALIA

Go one step further and destroy all things that tie you to the Lodge, such as aprons, rings, swords, pins, books, awards and tokens. We have a biblical example in Acts 19:19, where the early Christians renounced their religious heritage in idolatry and occultism by burning the scrolls used in sorcery. They made a complete break with their former religious practices. Masons who are seeking freedom in Christ should do the same.

You are a new person in Christ and the old has passed away (see 2 Cor. 5:17). Why hang on to these things? Move on! Former Masons and their families have informed me that they have greater victory once they sever *all* ties—emotional, spiritual and physical.

LETTER OF RESIGNATION

If you are or have been a Mason, you must further renounce Freemasonry by sending a letter of resignation to the Lodge. I have in my possession copies of letters of resignation, or what Masons refer to as demits, sent to me by Mike, the former Mason whose testimony you read in chapter 8. These letters include his demits from the Shrine Temple, the Masonic Lodge, the Scottish Rite of Freemasonry, the York Rite of Freemasonry and the Royal Arch Masons. (He was a busy man, wasn't he!) The following is the letter of resignation Mike sent to the Shrine Temple.

Dear Nobles and Brothers,

As a Christian member in good standing of this temple, I feel that I must honor the one true God and renounce my membership in this organization.

This was a very difficult decision for me to make as I have enjoyed many years of fellowship with the members of this group through the ——Shrine Club.

My love and concern for my fellow man has grown with my faith through active participation in a local church and extensive studies of the Bible. It is with this faith that I must act to withdraw my membership and warn my Christian brothers to repent, as we have committed a great sin before our God. Please read for yourselves the Scriptures in the Holy Bible:

Exodus 20:3 and Deuteronomy 5:7: "You shall have no other gods before me."

Exodus 23:13: "Be careful to do everything I have said to you. Do not invoke the names of other gods; do not let them be heard on your lips."

Deuteronomy 5:11: "You shall not misuse the name of the Lord your God, for the Lord will not hold anyone guiltless who misuses his name."

If you research the names of God, you will find that Allah is the name of another god! I am not a "true Moslem," but a follower of Jesus Christ, a "Christian." Further, there is no mention anywhere in the Bible of a prophet named Mohammed. He must, therefore, be [one of the] false prophets warned about throughout the Bible.[7]

I used to think that all of this kind of stuff was just for fun, a way for men to "let their hair down." I am now convinced that God takes all of this very seriously. I pray that God forgives us. Brothers, there is a spiritual battle taking place to turn our hearts away from the one true God. This [letter] is an effort on my part to remain faithful and a request for you to do the same.

Please read this letter in its entirety and grant my request for a demit at your next business meeting. My 1996 membership card is enclosed.

In God's great love,
Mike

In order to have a witnessing effect, these words must come from a heart of love and compassion. Pray that the Lord will give you the right heart and the right words. Keep in the forefront of your mind as you write that "our struggle is not against flesh and blood."[8] Your friends are also deceived and need to be set free from Freemasonry.

Deliverance Is Necessary to Get Free

The Hammonds remind us of a very important concept about deliverance from curses. They suggest that salvation does not automatically free us from curses, for many of God's children remain under curses even after they are born again.[9] Why? They have not *appropriated* Christ's redemption from the curses. Jesus died for all, but all are not saved. To come to salvation, a person must repent of his or her sin and appropriate—or claim—the blood of Jesus. Although Christ is the remedy for generational curses, we must personally repent for the sin that brought the curses and then renounce the curses and appropriate His blood over these curses.

CASTING OUT OR CASTING OFF

A minister friend of mine used to say: "When in doubt, cast it out." You may have heard leaders in the deliverance ministry use this phrase as well. In fact, I may have said it on occasion. Here's what we mean. If you even think you're being oppressed by demons, then just get rid of them! Now! Why let them hang around? God, through Jesus Christ, has made the provision for our complete freedom, so why not enjoy it? Now!

I'm certain that most people would agree that demon possession is scriptural. A brief scan of Christ's ministry should remove any doubt as to the reality of demon possession. Yet debate has persisted for centuries between theologians much wiser than this author regarding such questions as these: Who can have a demon? Can a person have demons and yet not be demon possessed? Is it possible for a Christian to have demons? I'm sure this debate will continue, but not in this book.

Suffice it to say, as I've traveled internationally, preaching and ministering deliverance, I've seen a lot that is difficult to understand—things that would seem to demolish the idea that Christians cannot have demons. But I can tell you that what I did see were very ugly manifestations in believers in Christ. These manifestations were not of the flesh, nor were they of God, which leads me to believe they were manifestations of demons. Again, this is only my viewpoint, and it comes not so much from what I've read but from what I've seen and experienced. The more I travel and teach, the more ministers I meet who concur with my findings.

Having said all that, I've also observed well-intentioned men and women trying desperately to cast demons out of a troubled person, yet no demons came out. The reason? There were no demons in the person. I must admit that at times I've done the same. Since then, I've discovered that to cast something out of a person is not always the same as to cast something off of that person. You see, occasionally it is not a matter of possession and thus casting something out; but rather, it is a case of oppression, and thus the deliverance seems to involve more of a casting off of the demonic. Put yet another way, the demonic curses didn't necessarily fall into the person; they fell upon them and need to be cast off.

Whether casting off or casting out, whether oppression or possession, deliverance from curses and bondages to demonic powers is still necessary to our spiritual freedom.

Now let's continue our journey to freedom from the curses of Freemasonry by praying a prayer of release for family members of Masons.

PRAYER OF RELEASE

This particular prayer of release from the curses of Freemasonry is taken from the book *Masonry: Beyond the Light.* Agree with me now as we pray:

> In the name of the Lord Jesus Christ, and by the authority I possess as a believer in Him, I declare that I am redeemed out of the hand of the devil. Through the blood of Jesus all my sins are forgiven. The blood of Jesus Christ, God's Son, is cleansing me right now from all sin. Through it I am righteous as if I have never sinned. Through the blood of Jesus I am sanctified, made holy, set apart for God and am a member of a chosen generation, a royal priesthood, holy nation, peculiar people, that I may show forth Your praises, Lord, who has called me out of darkness into Your marvelous light. My body is a temple of the Holy Spirit, redeemed and cleansed by the blood of Jesus. I belong to the Lord Jesus Christ, body, soul and spirit. His blood protects me from all evil.
>
> In Jesus' name I confess right now that my ancestors have been guilty of idolatry. I call that sin, and I ask Jesus to completely remove that sin from my life and the life of my family. In the name of Jesus I rebuke any and all lying and deceitful spirits of Freemasonry that may think they still have a claim on my family or me. In Jesus' name I renounce the spirits of Freemasonry and declare that they no longer have power over me. For I am bought and paid for by the blood of Jesus shed on Calvary. I renounce any and all oaths made at the altar of Freemasonry, in Jesus' holy name.

By the power of His shed blood I also break any generational curses and bondage that may be oppressing me by oaths made by my parents or ancestors. And I nail all these things to the cross of Christ. I also break any and all power of the devil of any oaths over my children or grandchildren and command them to leave them alone. For they are under the blood of the Lamb of God. Because of the blood of Jesus, Satan has no more power over me or my family and no place in us. I renounce him and his host completely and declare them my enemies.

Jesus said these signs shall follow them that believe: In My name they shall cast out devils. I am a believer, and in the name of Jesus I exercise my authority and expel all evil spirits. I command them to leave me right now, according to the Word of God and in the name of Jesus. Forgetting those things which are behind, and reaching forth for the things which are before me, I press toward the mark for the prize of the high calling of God in Christ Jesus. In Jesus' name, Amen.[10]

Just a couple of comments before closing. First, be sure to forgive those of your family who have bowed their knees at the altars of Freemasonry. The last thing you need is a heart of anger and bitterness toward those who opened the door to the curses that have visited your generation, for these emotions will surely hinder the blessings of God. Second, be sure to thank the Lord daily for His blessings and kindness. Don't linger in fear and doubt, for these are not of the Lord. Move on in faith, claiming the Scripture, "If the Son sets you free, you will be free indeed" (John 8:36).

In this book I have tried to communicate what I believe to be the truth concerning a deceiving, demonic spirit permeating an organization that purports to make good men better. I've also attempted to compassionately yet firmly show how Freemasonry, through its idolatrous rituals, brings very real bondage and curses upon Masons and their families. Finally, I led you through the "What can we do about it?" chapters, and the prayers of repentance and release.

I recognize it may have been an arduous journey for some, so I thank you for courageously remaining with me as we threw off the bondage of Egypt, so to speak, and pressed on into the Promised Land of complete freedom in Christ.

May God bless you and your family abundantly as you remain free from Freemasonry.

Ron G. Gampbell
445 C East Cheyenne Mountain Blvd., #241
Colorado Springs, CO 80906

Notes
1. Albert Mackey, *An Encyclopedia of Freemasonry*, Vol. 2 (New York: The Masonic History Company, 1915), p. 126.
2. C. Peter Wagner, *The Power to Change the Past* (Pasadena, Calif.: Global Harvest Ministries, n.d.), introduction, p. 3.
3. See Exodus 20:5, 34:7; Leviticus 26:39,40; Numbers 14:18, 18:1; Deuteronomy 5:9; Psalm 106:6, 109:14, Isaiah 14:21; Jeremiah 2:5, 14:20, 32:18.
4. Wagner, *The Power to Change the Past*, p. 6
5. Ibid.
6. Ezekiel 18:4.
7. I've been told by Shriners that the *Koran*, or the *Volume of Sacred Law of the Moslems*, is on the altar at the time of the candidate's initiation into the Shrine. Also, there are references to Allah as god in the Shrine. This is what prompted Mike to include terms such as "Allah" and "Mohammed" in his letter of resignation.
8. See Ephesians 6:12.
9. Frank and Ida Mae Hammond, *The Breaking of Curses* (Plainview, Tex.: Impact Books, 1993), p. 82.
10. Bill Schnoebelen, *Masonry: Beyond the Light* (Chino, Calif.: Chick Publications, 1991), pp. 268-270.

SUGGESTED READING

This bibliography is not a complete record of all the works and sources I have consulted. It indicates the substance and range of reading upon which I have formed my ideas.

Ankerberg, John, and Weldon, John. *The Secret Teachings of the Masonic Lodge.* Chicago: Moody Press, 1990.

Breasted, James Henry. *A History of Egypt.* New York: Charles Scribner's Sons, 1905.

Casavis, J. N. *The Greek Origin of Freemasonry.* New York: D. C. Divry, 1955.

Coleman, Rev. Henry R. *Light from the East.* Louisville, Ky.: Knight & Leonard, 1881.

Duncan, Malcolm C. *Duncan's Ritual of Freemasonry.* New York: David McKay Company, n.d.

Finney, Charles. *Character and Claims of Freemasonry.* Chicago: Ezra A. Cook & Co., 1879.

Hannah, Walton. *Darkness Visible.* London: Augustine Press, 1952.

Holly, M.D., James L. *A Report on Freemasonry,* Home Missions Board, Southern Baptist Convention. Taylors, S.C.: Faith Printing Company, 1993.

Knapp, Esq., Samuel L., and Redding, Moses W. "The Genius of Masonry," *The Illustrated History of Free Masonry*. New York: Redding & Co., 1901.

Mackey, Albert G. *An Encyclopedia of Freemasonry*, 2 vols. New York: The Masonic History Company, 1915.

_____. *Masonry Defined*. Memphis, Tenn.: Masonic Supply Co., 1925.

MacKenzie, Norman. *Secret Societies*. London: Aldus Books Limited, 1967.

MacNulty, W. Kirk. *Freemasonry, A Journey Through Ritual and Symbol*. New York: Thames and Hudson, 1991.

Macoy, Robert. *A Dictionary of Freemasonry*. New York: Bell Publishing Co., 1989.

Microsoft® Encarta® 96 Encyclopedia. The American Heritage Dictionary, third edition copyright© 1994 by Houghton Mifflin Company. Electronic version licensed from and portions copyright© 1994 by INSO Corporation. All rights reserved.

Morris, Robert. *Freemasonry in the Holy Land*. New York: Masonic Publishing Company, 1875.

Newton, Joseph. *The Builders: A Story and Study of Freemasonry*. New York: Macoy Publishers and Masonic Supply Co., 1951.

The NIV Study Bible, New International Version. Grand Rapids, Mich.: Zondervan Publishing House, 1985.

Pike, Albert. *Morals and Dogma of the Ancient and Accepted Scottish Rite of Freemasonry.* Richmond, Va.: L. H. Jenkins, 1947.

Redding, Moses W. *The Illustrated History of Freemasonry.* New York: Redding & Co., 1901.

Roberts, Allen E. *The Mystic Tie.* Richmond, Va.: Macoy Publishing & Masonic Supply Co., 1988.

Ronayne, Edmond. *The Master's Carpet.* Chicago: Ezra A. Cook Publications, 1959.

Shaw, James D., and McKenney, Tom C. *The Deadly Deception.* Lafayette, La.: Huntington House, 1988.

Short, Martin. *Inside the Brotherhood.* New York: Dorset Press, 1989.

Spence, Lewis. *Encyclopedia of Occultism.* New Hyde Park, N.Y.: University Books, 1960.

Stillson, Henry Leonard, ed. *History of the Ancient and Honorable Fraternity of Free and Accepted Masons.* London: The Fraternity Publishing Company, 1921.

Whitsell, Leon O., Past Grand Master. *One Hundred Years of Freemasonry in California.* San Francisco, Calif.: Grand Lodge, Free and Accepted Masons of California, 1950.

Wilmshurst, W. L. *The Meaning of Masonry.* New York: Gramercy Books, 1980.